# CREATING AND MAINTAINING SUCCESS

"Success is a process, must be earned, and is not a given."

BY JIM VILLELLA

## Dedication

Only through what I learned from Charlie Birkholz, is this book possible. From the beginning of our co-authored book, *If You Ain't the Lead Dog, the Scenery Never Changes*, (later named "The Battle to Stay Competitive") did I learn what it takes to create a book that may be interesting enough for the reader to learn and apply something from the book's content.

# Contents

## Prologue

From the *Webster's 7th New Collegiate Dictionary* dated 1971, "Success" can be defined as:

- A favorable termination of a venture
- Attainment of wealth, favor, or eminence
- One that succeeds

From *Wikipedia in 2016,* "Success" can be defined as:

- The accomplishment of an aim or purpose
- A favorable outcome
- A gain in popularity
- A recognition of prominence
- Attainment of prosperity, affluence, wealth, and riches

If you ask a large number of people what they mean by the definition of "Success", most but not all will reply with a comment that has something to do with the subject of wealth.

I think the definition of "Success" encompasses all of the definitions above with equal weight. By that I mean that not one definition is more important or more correctly defines the word "Success" than the other. It all comes down to who you ask, or what reference you use for your definition.

If you look at *Wikipedia's* definitions closely, I think that you may convince yourself with the following examples:

- The accomplishment of an aim or purpose: "I finished first"

- A favorable outcome: "I won and beat all others"
- A gain in popularity: "I was elected Homecoming Queen above all other candidates"
- A recognition of prominence: "I was elected president to a high political office"
- Attainment of prosperity, affluence, wealth, and riches: "AKA Net Worth or being a multi-millionaire or even by today's standards a billionaire"

One other concept came to my mind. I have known a lot of successful people in my life that had accomplished much, had won many times, were very popular, had experienced many favorable outcomes, and were wealthy. But very few people knew anything about them, so they never gained the recognition of other "well known" individuals that had gained that same level of "Success."

Years ago, my dad told me, "If you steal a nickel, you will lose a dime later on in life, but you will have no idea why." Now, my dad may not have been defined as a "Success" by any of the definitions previously mentioned. He was born in Italy and came to America at the age of 14. After his arrival, he was put in the 2nd grade at the local Catholic grade school, since he could not speak English. I can just imagine his "normal" day at school, being 14 years old, with all 2nd graders, and not speaking English. The other kids probably made fun of him at times. He left school after 2 years and went to work in a local paper

v

mill. He worked his way up to becoming a foreman at that plant. A "Success" in my mind.

Also about the same time, my mom told me, "If you give someone a nickel, you will receive a quarter later on in life, but you will have no idea why." My mom's educational background was a little different story. She was born in a small rural town in Kentucky, called Jenkins. She graduated from high school and then made a decision to go to Ohio, where there was much more opportunity for employment. Based on educational backgrounds, my mom could be considered more of a "Success" than my dad.

Both gave me outstanding information to live by, which of course I completely ignored. My thought was, what do parents really know? Basically a lot of good, no great information, is not always absorbed by a teenager's mind. Can anyone out there relate to this?

I guess the real reason for this book is to "shine some light" on individuals who may have not been well known or successful, just because they were not famous athletes, screen stars, or public figures.

There are 2 reasons why I collected the individual stories of successful individuals who may not be at that level as famous athletes, screen stars, and public figures. First, I think you will find it interesting that the successful people I know come from a variety of backgrounds and socioeconomic levels and still attain a degree of success. Second, I am looking for a "common thread" or what do all successful people have in common with one another? Is there a recipe for success? I hope that you, the reader, can relate to other such individuals that have in some way attained some level of success, but no one knows about them.

This book was made possible by 3 things. First, family, friends, and neighbors, who actually had "Success" in their lives that allowed me to publish their stories. Second, the manuscript being proofread by my wife, Kim. I want everyone to know this because to accomplish this task she had to put up with the training of a 4 month old cocker spaniel puppy and a husband who kept asking her every 30 minutes about "grammar rules." Third, the complete formatting of the book by Rich and Mary Anne Miletic, prior to going to the publisher. Both Rich and Mary Anne had the ability to take all of what I generated from the chapter authors, proofread by Kim, and transform it into something that the publisher would accept!

One final comment. This is a nontraditional book. By that I mean you will notice that the chapters vary greatly in length. Some had little to say to express their success, others had more to say. My intent was to give each chapter's authors complete creative freedom to communicate their message.

All proceeds from this book will be donated to Chandler, Arizona local charities. Reason being, at my age (over 70) I am trying to follow my dad and mom's advice. Some of us are "slow learners."

**Billy Serrano**
**Business Field:** Restaurant Management
**Business Name:** Serranos
**Current Position:** Vice-President Restaurant Operations

## Personal Background:

I graduated from Chandler High School in Chandler, Arizona in 1988. I started working for the "Business" in 1983 part-time during school. My responsibilities included, but were not limited to, dish washing, busing, hosting and various maintenance duties. Since I was underage, no serving or bartending was part of my routine. What I learned from this experience was that I was a decent employee, but not a "model" employee.

I think the "Whats" of my success started right after graduation, I went to work for Bashas' Warehouse. My responsibilities there included fork lift driver, warehousing items, order picker, maintenance and any labor required to do anything anywhere.

In 1992, I came into the family business of Serranos Mexican Restaurants. During this time I was involved in management training, which included working in the positions of: prep cook, dish washing, serving, hosting, and bartending. During my tenure here, I learned how to "manage" people. By experiencing each department, I also learned the meaning of expectations and of meeting expectations. At first I did not take the concept of expectation seriously. But when I became manager of our Chandler location, I felt that since I had "walked in the shoes" of the employees, I had an

1

advantage of knowing what was going through their minds with the new "Boss." One thing that I had going for me as a new manager, was that the restaurant location was profitable when I got there.

When I became the manager, I brought the "Green House" approach of managing. By this I mean that I was managing older employees who were much more experienced than me. I tried to listen to their reasoning about how to do things. I tried not to "look down" on anyone, always be humble, and never thought that anyone was ever beneath me. During my stint at this location, I tried to set an example by doing all the things that I was asking my employees to do, such as "plunging" toilets, mopping up spills, and picking up trash that some customers left behind. My thought was trying to teach and lead by example.

One of the greatest lessons learned in my life has been listening to the Customer. If you look at all complaints as just a complaint, you lose the opportunity to make things better. If you can make a Customer's experience better, no matter what the source of the problem, they win and you win. One of my favorites is that you will have a customer who is a "known complainer." Since not many of your employees, including yours do not like the customer, never forget to listen to that customer as they may bring up something that is really important to your business. Your other "good" customers may not communicate that information to you, which could be helpful.

"Thinking on my feet" was a concept that I had to learn. Each day of your life, you may be thrown a curve ball, when you were expecting a fastball. When I first took over as a manager, I had an assistant that been with the company a number of years. Then she moved on, and I had to hire another assistant manager. When taking on new managers, I tried to remember a number of things. First, since my last name was Serrano, my name was on the building. I also had boundaries as the Manager. As an assistant manager, we sometimes promoted from within. Based on that decision, the assistant manager may have had close ties to the current employees who they are managing as they probably had worked with the current restaurant's employees or another one of our restaurant's employees. It takes a special relationship to be promoted from within, have friends now working for you, and maybe not being their best friend anymore. I had to learn how to handle these types of relationships between myself, my assistant, and others to provide quality service to the customer.

Another important concept that has led to our success, was my 5 other siblings. Each had a vital part in the business. My brother Ric is the current COE, my sister Theresa is head of HR, Stephanie is head of Accounts Payable, Ernie is VP of Restaurant Operations, and Lorraine is head of Kitchen Operations.

Ric is responsible for bringing in new employees to our restaurants. His criteria for becoming a Serrano employee is based on the following:

- Experience in any type of restaurant
- Experiences in dealing with people in many types of situations

- Asking for a potential employee's reply to different scenarios that they may come up against in their employment with Serranos
- Questions relating to how they can "think on their feet"
- Evaluating their educational background to see if it enhances them as potential employee. A minimum of a high school education is a primary expectation
- Experiences of prior work
- References from others

I was at the Chandler restaurant for about 3 years. After leaving that location, I was assigned to the McKellips & Gilbert Road location, which was opened in 1992. I stayed at that location until 1995. We then opened our Dobson location in 1994, where I was assigned as the Manager. I had a decent "stretch" at this location where I learned that I had to deal with employee situations. I realized that I had reached a point where I had to put my foot down, so to speak.

In 1995, I was managing the Mesa location and it was a good store. It had a great location in a pavilion which had very few ordinances, and there was a lot of activity in that location. That location was doing at times what our McKellips & Gilbert Road location was doing.

Our location at Dobson and Guadalupe started on a severe decline in sales right around the time the State of Arizona put in the Mesa "No Smoking Ordinance." Because of this and a decline in demographics, we ended up closing this location in 2014.

We currently have 7 locations (6 Mexican restaurants + Brunchies Breakfast & Lunch) and I have worked at all of them. Since maintenance was my Dad's field of work, I took over for him when he became ill in 2005. I have been on the Serranos maintenance end of the restaurant business ever since. Customers never see the maintenance aspect of a restaurant. What they see is, is my food order correct, am I being served what I ordered, and probably most importantly is my bill correct! What the Customer does not see is the "process" behind them being satisfied with their order.

For the Customer to be satisfied there is a sequence of events that takes place. It starts with the waiter/waitress taking the order correctly, communicating that order to the kitchen by a piece of paper or through a computerized order system, the receipt of the correct information into the kitchen, the inventory of "food stuff" to support their on hand inventory, the proper preparation of that food, the delivery of that food, to the server, and finally the delivery of that order to the customer. If for any reason that series of events becomes broken, the customer is dissatisfied. I have also heard that if you have a satisfied customer they may tell one other person. If you have a dissatisfied customer they will tell 10 people. With today's social media, it takes only seconds to communicate a bad dining experience and more than 10 people will know about it!

I think that the "Hows" of my success can be attributed to a number of items. The first being my dad. He loved me as a son which I can't really put into words. What my dad did for me, I try to do for my son. What my dad did not do for me, I try to do for my son. Since my dad was involved in the maintenance side of the business, he had irregular hours. As one can imagine, equipment does not always break down between the hours of 7:30 am and 4:00 pm.

Since I am somewhat tied to an around the clock schedule and weekends, I try and take the opportunity to spend that "open window" time with my wife and son. Being involved in my son's scouts, sports at school, knowing his friends and more importantly, his friend's parents, has allowed me to devote "quality time" to the business and all of our employees. This closeness has allowed us to monitor any negative behaviors of our son and his friends. Remember, a bad situation at home creates a bad situation at work, and vice versa.

Another item that has led to my success is that my parents did not shield their kids from negative events in our lives. When someone passed, my parents took the opportunity to explain why someone had died. This was viewed as an opportunity for them to explain life as a cycle from beginning to end. Too many times we try to shield our spouse, our kid(s) and employees from bad news. As most of us understand, life is not always fair. But, when we experience a negative event, learn from it, and apply life's lessons to future situations. An example is our kitchen equipment, as it always breaks down during the "rush hours." I guess there may be some truth to planned maintenance vs reactive maintenance.

In the area of "Giving Back," for the past 11 years I have been a sacristan at St. Mary's. This experience has allowed me to learn about serving others and taking care of one another. I try to apply these same principles to the business. People are people, no matter what the environment. I learned years ago that short term the tyrant may get a few things accomplished quickly and make a big splash in the eyes of a few. But, long term compassion with well communicated expectations will carry you much further towards making the business a success.

Another area is being an active member of the Cursillo Movement. This is a 3 ½ day retreat that I have attended since 2003. Cursillos in Christianity is a movement within the church that, through a method of its own tries to, and through God's grace manages to, enable the essential realities of the Christian to come to life in the uniqueness, originality, and creativity of each person.

In becoming aware of their potential and while accepting their limitations they exercise their freedom by their conviction, strengthen their will with their decision, to propitiate friendship in virtue of their constancy in both their personal and community life. What this event has helped me to understand and apply to family and business is from a weekend retreat, it allowed me to deal with all my challenges within my business family as well as my personal l family. By working at one of these retreats you can step back and take a view of many. You can see all personal changes that are taking place within a group. You can see these same changes taking place in your business, because people are people, wherever they are. At work or at home, the process is still the same.

I see the power of words and prayer. Linkage from the Cussillo experience to Serranos helps you talk to people. There is a level of compassion that helps you draw the line in a corporate way. It also allowed me not to shield my faith, so people would never question who I am or what I am.

In my dad's later years, my mom was not strong enough and had to have assistance. As a family we decided to get her "outside" assistance. We thought that was the right thing to do. But my dad became very upset that with 8 kids in the family, could we not figure out how to provide support and care without hiring someone from the outside? Since it definitely was not a financial decision of not being able to afford outside assistance, my siblings and I decided to take the assistance of my mom into our own hands.

Since my dad and mom were involved in a department store for 20 years and then the restaurant business, it became a very difficult time in their lives when they could no longer function as they had for so many years.

It became almost a blessed opportunity for us to be able to assist our parents, to "give back" to two people that gave so much to us. Since my mom can no longer communicate, we have learned many valuable lessons that can be applied to my own family and my extended family at work. I know that they are all facing the same or similar issues in their lives. Since I am walking in their same shoes, I feel that I can help.

Giving back to my dad was a humbling experience for me and my siblings. Dad felt much more comfortable and because his life was positively affected, which had a positive effect on all of our lives, as it was a win-win. This paved the way to take care of my mother and we all made the transition much easier.

We all know what is right and wrong. I think that people allow "wrong" if they allow the "right" feelings inside them not to be used on a daily basis. This has a positive boost effect to one's family and business. "Giving Back" is a process, which allows people of success to assist and maintain a support level of individuals or groups that can't provide for themselves.

Another area for giving back is the Knights of Columbus, which is fairly new to me. I believe that it is a good driving force for our new Church St. Juan Diego. My grandfather was a Grand Knight, my dad a Knight, my uncle a Knight and my brother a 4th Knight. This area has become a new part of me as an active member.

I want everyone to know that this is just a "snippet" of our family story. Much more could be said, but I think that you get the idea of what I do and why I do it.

**Carrie Fassion**
**Business Field:** Residential Real Estate
**Business Name:** My Home Group Realty
**Current Position:** Realtor® GRI, CSSPE

## Personal Background:

I was born and raised in Denver, Colorado. My mom and dad were Richard Ruhland and Patricia O'Neill. As you may guess, my dad was of German heritage and my mom Irish. I have 1 Sister, Kathy and 2 Brothers, Rick and Rob.

I attended Arapahoe High School, and was involved in a specialty chorus group of 9 members. I also participated on our speech and debate teams. I did not attend college; instead I married my high school sweetheart, Lon Faison and have a wonderful, loving family consisting of 3 children and 10 grandchildren.

My sister, who is 1 year older than I, went to college, completed her master's degree and was the perfect child who followed in my dad's footsteps focused on having a professional life. I always compared myself to her, and that left me with feelings of being very inadequate in my father's eyes. You see, my father was a perfectionist, very controlling with a powerful presence. He was a passionate man in all that he did. He and my mother instilled the highest moral values in my brothers, my sister, and me. He always said, "Be truthful, always be the best in what you choose to do, and never give up! If you start something, finish it-no exceptions, no excuses!"

My mom was the nurturer who always told us to be kind to others and "Do unto others as you would have them do unto you." My dad was brilliant, (He was actually one of the original "whiz kids"). If you took him to Las Vegas, he could count the cards dealt before the dealer could! My mom supported all his decisions. Going back to my dad, he ruled with an iron hand. That is not to say that he did not love us, because he did. He was also an excellent provider for his family. My dad's values were instilled in me at an early age, and today I am so very grateful!

My first job as a teenager was working at a department store. Little did I know this would be my start working with the public. This job enabled me to learn how to communicate with lots of different types of people at all educational and emotional levels. I did not realize it at the time, but that first work experience would come in very handy later in life.

My second job was working in a grocery store bakery. I was waiting on the public once again. This taught me that communication, persistence, and good listening skills while working with others, was not only important, but had to be performed with a smile, too! I learned to be a negotiator, communicator, and a great listener. I never got intrusive in anyone's life, but I always had the ability to get more from people, to make them feel comfortable, and you know what, they left smiling too! They didn't know it, but what I did for them during our interaction was me giving back to them!

My third job was working for the school system. My husband and I have 3 children, Kristine, Shawn and Angela. This job allowed me to have the same school hours as my children's school schedule, with no day care so no "latch key" kids in this family. My goal was always to be a great mom, a great wife, and like my dad and mom, to instill those same values I was taught as a child. I was very fortunate to have a husband that provided for us, took an active part in raising our family, and who never asked me to get a job. He always supported me, and still does support me 100%. I started out as a teacher's aide in my children's elementary school and found that I not only interacted with the children and their teachers, but with the parents too.

My last 8 years were spent in the middle school next door to the high school as the assistant to the librarian. This was really cool for my high school children. Since the middle school was across from the high school, they could come over for report materials, or if they needed me to sign their permission slip I was close by, or usually they needed money for lunch.

My husband and I gave all 3 of our children the opportunity to go to college. Today they are all very successful in the lives they chose for themselves, and as my son said to us one day, "You were very strict parents but fair!" All 3 of our children continue to thank us, and they tell us every day that they are who they are and the way they are, because of us!

Now to my career after my children flew the nest. I started out as a real estate assistant. My duties were that of an office manager, taking care of all the broker's files, and doing so for an hourly wage. I took notice, listening and learning from the company staff and agents and decided that this was something I could do! I quickly made the decision to go to a real estate school and begin my new career. Those words my dad said to me, "Success and failure exist in the power of the mind," helped me set my goals and I took off in my new career!

In my mind, I had to create a strategy, be persistent, make sure that I watched, and learned everything I could. Remember those words, "Do the best that you can, keep your feet on the ground," taught by my dad. He was the one that gave me the tools for success in my career and my life!

Today I am passionate, and I want everything to be perfect, (oh boy this is my dad all over again)! It is in my mental make up to be this way. In my mind, success and failure exist in the power of your mind. If you don't think this way, most likely you will not be successful. Why, because you don't have faith in yourself!

You need to have that picture of success in your mind. If you can see it, you can do it. I think that too many times, people can't visualize the "successful picture" just because of the inability to think they can be great at something! I had to build "Carrie Faison the Professional REALTOR®" from the ground up. I had to build a foundation from which to launch my career.

It is also important to align yourself with successful people. Build yourself a network of people who share your own values. Too many times people see success as something they can't achieve. They do not investigate how others got there. A method I used was to network with successful people. I would go to charitable affairs, networking activities, and talk with many communication coordinators. I found that communication coordinators have the ability to reach many people.

13

This ability became a strength for me to reach out to potential clients in the real estate world.

Earlier, as I mentioned, I had it drilled into me to watch, listen, and learn. You must also set goals. I would set a goal to beat my productivity from the year before, and I still do it. One of my goals was to become a multi-million dollar sales agent. I have also attained that goal.

Along with a goal, it is imperative that you have a Mission Statement. My Mission Statement is:

*"To facilitate my client's dreams to either sell or buy the homes of their choice and to provide superior service to every client - through every transaction - every time."*

Let's now look at how offering "Clear Value" to all of my clients' works. When I am interacting with all of my clients, they all clearly know what I am offering. I do not beat around the bush. I don't mince words. What comes out of these 2 concepts is a trusting relationship, and they will always know where Carrie stands on any issue. My clients say," I like you and I like knowing what you are about. "You have made me very comfortable making this decision with your knowledge and professionalism." The world is not perfect, business is not perfect. I prepare for each of my clients and preparation is everything. There is a solution or answer to everything that might come along.

How have I gotten to where I am in my real estate career? I believed in myself. It was not only a new career, but a risk (could I do this?). I had to really believe in me and apply myself. I know I keep saying this, but I listened and learned. I was like a sponge, absorbing all the information. I used all of this to help myself become successful.

Remember, I was the quiet sibling. I took a back seat and didn't make waves in the family. I will never forget the time that my sister and I (as young teenagers) met these 2 neighbor boys. After my sister finished talking to them, one of them said to my sister, "Does your sister talk?" I was horrified, but I realized I hadn't said one word!

I started by letting my family, friends, and everyone else know that, "I am a Realtor now. So if you need, or know of anyone in need of a REALTOR, let me know. Please have them call me." I think most realtors usually take a similar approach to get started. This is the first thing that you do; it's called building a database. Marketing and networking comes in after that. This database builds referrals that bring business back to you. I want others, those I haven't even met yet, to hear from all my clients, "I have got a great realtor for you."

In this business success is knowing your client's needs, to think like the client, to create an outstanding business relationship, a relationship based on trust, knowledge, professionalism and the personal qualities your clients want from your business. Creating a great relationship will carry you very, very far in this business. Use the tools of your business, feedback from the clients and other professionals. Don't take NO for an answer. You can solve problems and seek resolutions. You learn to persuade fellow optimists to become more pro-active and ignore the criticism of pessimists.

I have gained so much business sense from feedback and experiences from others in this business. These are the title companies and the mortgage lenders. They work with others in my type of business, they see what has worked, and I ask that they share their knowledge with me. Having a great relationship with them has allowed me to grow personally as well as professionally. This has allowed me to do what I do better. These professionals are the business tools or partners that assist me in my business. They have ideas and business thoughts that they share with me. They will say, "Carrie have you tried this or how about doing it this way?" I'm open for all suggestions and anything that will benefit my business and my clients.

Another very important factor in this business is the art of negotiation. I look at it this way; if you have an issue that looks like it is stopping a deal, can you find another item or items that may outweigh the negative issue holding up the sale? You bet! You ask your client, "How important is this or that to you? Is it a deal killer?" The way you deal with this one negative can turn the deal into a positive. Again, it is about negotiation and never forgetting about your client's needs.

Your discussion with your client, on how can we improve our position means always working together. My client and I always have that final goal in mind for a successful sale. Bottom line, good communication that goes back and forth leads to the strong relationship that carries you far, that means referrals and repeat business will come my way, and that is what sets you above all your peers.

Let's face it, this business is Public Service. If I do not give the right type of service, who will use me in the future? Who is going to say that Carrie Faison is the best realtor I've ever worked with and the best REALTOR for you!

Marketing your business means marketing yourself and putting yourself out there. You must have a conduit between yourself and potential clients. This might be the use of the Internet and all the other social media tools, such as the use of post office mailers. You must market yourself. I just had a gentleman (as an example) attend one of my open houses. I could tell he was not really wanting to give me a lot of information about himself or share any personal information with me, or commit to anything, but continued asking many questions, which I gladly answered. He worked his way to the front door and as he was leaving I said, "Let me give you my card!" He stopped and said that he didn't need my card because he had one of my mailer's at home on his refrigerator.

That told me that the marketing in this community has really paid off. I know my communication is working. When networking or just performing daily activities, I will run into someone who will say, "Oh yes, I know you, you are Carrie Faison the Realtor. I get your cards in the mail all of the time. I was just referred to you by a friend, a past client of yours, who said it was a pleasure to work with you, and how easy it was to work with you, because of your professionalism and knowledge of your business!" This is the greatest gift that I could ask of my clients, that they write a letter of recommendation about their business experience with me so that I can share this with other sellers and buyers in my future.

17

Our Realtor Code of Ethics says, "When representing a buyer, seller, landlord, tenant, or other client, as an agent, pledge themselves to protect and promote the interests of their client." We work for the client and the client's needs, it's not about us, but about them. That means that I am working for a successful transaction for all parties. Nothing is to stand in the way of working for these parties to ensure a successful transaction, the closing of a property. That's the way it should be and that is the way I run my business!

I've "Given Back" throughout my life. I was a PTO president, classroom volunteer, Cub Scout leader, and religious education teacher. I deliver meals to those who cannot leave their homes and participate in many other community volunteer activities.

I am thankful for my Faith in God. I pray every day for my family, friends, and my clients, and all those in need. I thank God for all the blessings in my life, starting with my parents and how they raised me, my husband, and our children and how they are raising their families today. Our health, and yes, I thank God for my business too.

Right in line with this, is the good old USA where we live with our freedoms to enjoy all of what I have spoken about in this Chapter. I am thankful for the way that I turned out to be.

**Charlie King**
**Business Field:** Small Business Growth Coach
**Business Name:** Charlie King Coaching
**Current Position**: Founder and President

## Personal Background:

I was born in Boston, Massachusetts. I spent my formative years growing up in the Boston area and lived in Cambridge, Massachusetts, right outside of Harvard Square, near Harvard University. I had two college educated parents. I had one brother and my parents cared a great deal about us. One of the things that was a hallmark of my growing up, was growing up with parents that struggled with their relationship with themselves.

I grew up in a family where there were a lot of expectations. Expectations that my behavior would meet my parents' expectations *and* the expectations of others. It wasn't uncommon for my mother to express disappointment or be upset that we weren't measuring up to her perception of the expectations of others. A completely moving target of expectations we could not predict. This pattern made me extremely good at being "quick on my feet," and being able to meet expectations of others. It made me a really effective "chameleon." It made me believe that all of life was lived in performance and that not all that much was really authentic. I also learned some amazing skills that allow me to fit in almost anywhere with ease. Some of these skills have served me well over time and some behaviors have been to my detriment as well.

I was the younger of two boys. My brother was a big personality. He was big in lots of different ways. But he had some struggles through his teen years. My parents were always trying to figure out the best way to support and manage him. While this was going on, I tried to stay under the radar, the safest place to be. Being under the radar, no one was noticing me. This led my parents to believe "Charlie must be okay because we don't hear from him."

When I was in my 20s, my mother revealed to me in a conversation, that there were a number of people that knew me, who were waiting to find out who I was. I was spending so much time being my elder brother's "little brother" that they really don't know who Charlie is. This revelation hit me like a hammer. Here I was in my 20s discovering that important people in my life knew me as somebody who lived in the shadow of someone else, without definition.

The formative experiences I have had in my life that changed things pretty dramatically for me had nothing to do with my education. The first of which was when my parents were getting divorced and I was probably 16 years old. It was a struggle for both of my parents while they were trying to move through this process. My mom decided to go and attend a program called Landmark Education. They specialized in exploring how we're hard wired for some things, and revealing patterns we live in. Patterns including how we see each other and ourselves. When she came out of this program, she was radiant. I had never seen her like this before. This experience had made such a huge difference for her. It was like a heaviness had been lifted. Then she invited me, at the encouragement of others in the program, to come in and see her graduation.

She was so lit up about this program, and based on her experience, I asked her if I could take this program. The reason being is that I saw something in her that I did not see in myself. I wanted to see if I could get access to the same experience. So, I took this very intensive program and something opened up in me that I had never even had a concept that was available before. For the first time I saw a way of being and interacting with the world, where I got to say how things went for me. So regardless of what was happening on the outside, I got to have some say on what goes on in the inside with me. This was a remarkable awareness. What came from this was a real sense of power and a sense of lightness, too.

It certainly had an impact on what happened when I left high school. I moved out west to California for a year. I was an intern at the Monterey Bay Aquarium during a gap year before college. This was an incredible maturing and informative experience for me. The reason for my gap of a year between high school and college was the perception of the adults in my life (correctly so) that I wasn't mature enough for college yet. It was an amazing experience. I was thrown into adult life and loved it. Three thousand miles from home, a job that was amazing, and living in a beautiful place.

I had to find a place to live, a roommate, had to be responsible for my own schedule, and could create myself as anyone that I wanted. I shed the shell of the insecure heavyset high school kid in favor of a more authentic self. The aquarium did not have a program for interns when I arrived. I was their first. They gave me a set of uniforms and a set of keys and

21

sent me to work all over the aquarium. It was one of the most memorable years of my life. My year away was filled working with adults, scuba diving, and just having some wide open freedom. It was really a formative piece in my life.

When I went to college after that year off, it was almost like I was a different person. Everything just seemed so easy after living "out in the world." Everything seemed to be so straightforward in college. All you had to do was show up for class, for meals, and do your homework. They provided your housing, your entertainment, and everything else you could either take or leave. So to me, college was really straightforward.

Four years in Chicago earned me my BA in Political Science. I distinctly remember during my junior year one of my classmates asked me what my plan was with my political science major. I said I didn't know, suddenly realizing I was clueless of needing a plan for my major. My friend then shared with me that my major was the path for many future lawyers and politicians. This was a wake up moment for me because it was clear there was no future for me as a lawyer or a politician.

I was ready for my next challenge and adventure. So after graduation, I departed for Wyoming to attend a course at the National Outdoors Leadership School (NOLS). This program is a month long leadership and outdoor skills training program in the Wind River Mountain range. I spent a month living a self-sustained existence while hiking and learning about back country camping, cooking, orienteering (map reading and compass use), fishing, climbing, and exploring. From sustainability to survival, from mountaineering to mushroom identification, from knot tying to navigating, it was an amazing experience. This program opened up a whole new arena of what was possible and what I was capable of doing.

I learned that I was capable of so much more than just taking care of myself. It put the questions of "Am I going to make it?" and "Where am I going in my life?" by the wayside. After my program I had planned to return to Massachusetts and move in with my fiancé and begin my "adult life" in New England. Wyoming changed me. The Rockies, the West in general had so much more possibility and adventure that I couldn't imagine not moving there. I invited my fiancé at the time to come with me. I shared with her that I would totally understand if she did not want to come with me, but if she decided not to go, I was going anyway.

Probably a month later, with the car packed, my fiancé and I moved out to Santa Fe, New Mexico. The trip lasted as long as the remainder of our relationship once we arrived. About a month and a half after our arrival, she decided to move back to Massachusetts.

I spent a decade in New Mexico, where I met my wife of 20 years (so far!) and further tilling and planting the soil of experience. In Santa Fe I worked service jobs in the tourist industry; the most memorable was working for Paul Reindorf. His small electronics repair business for Paul's analytical perspective, willingness to question the status quo and think outside the box made him an amazing man to work under, especially in light of the small size of his business. He had half a dozen employees at 2 or

3 locations. His curiosity and approach to problems and issues was really eye opening. He knew that there was not just one way, but a 100 ways to address an issue. Watching him craft which way he wanted to go and how he was going to either sell it, pitch it, or share it was part creativity and part personal expression. It was amazing to behold.

After working in small businesses for a while, I discovered that there was not all that much that I wanted to do in Santa Fe for a living. There was really no living to be made in the outdoors. It was a beautiful place to go and play, but it was hard to make a living there. So I ended up wandering into emergency medicine. I started volunteering with the Santa Fe Fire Department. I found that I had a real passion in being a volunteer. There was so much to learn about the equipment and technology. There was a lot of training and lots of committed people involved.

Every time I volunteered within the department, I found out that I was the youngest volunteer in the department, by more than 10 years. It soon became evident that since I was the youngest and had the most energy of any of the volunteers, the fire chief encouraged me to step up and become more involved. He would give me something and I would become trained in it. Then when I was done, I would walk up to him and ask what is next? We got to a point where I was proficient in firefighting skills that were required by the department. The Chief said that the reality was that most calls had to do with medical emergencies, so what he suggested was that I should get trained as an EMT.

So I went off to EMT school and then started playing in that arena. Getting into medicine was a field I had never played in or had knowledge about. I was learning how to care for others. NOLS taught me how to take care of myself and now I was learning how to care for others. In relative short order I found myself being hired on by an ambulance company. I was then volunteering in my off time and working full time as an EMT for a local ambulance company.

After this, I made a transition to go to paramedic school. I would spend 3 days a week going to school 3 hours' drive from home. Then, I would commute back and work full-time the other 4 days. This was an "out of the pan into the fire" type of experience for me. I was doing emergency medicine all the time. Everything that I learned, I was implementing at work. This experience made me incredibility competent pretty quickly, but it also almost ended my career as soon as it started. This was because by the time I had graduated from school as a paramedic, I was burned out. Seventy hour weeks over an 18 month period were just too much for me.

Within a year, the service director of the ambulance company that I was working for, and also the owner of the company, decided to move out of the state. He offered me the Chief Operating Officer's position. I accepted and spent a year in that position, managing a $10 million dollar ambulance company. I soon discovered that this was not the right role for me. I really missed doing direct care. I did not want the responsibility of "owning" the entire business, because that is really what the job was, regardless of what the job description said. The expectation was that you run the entire business.

My daughter was born in December of 2000. My wife and I decided that even before our daughter was born, we were going to leave Santa Fe. A lot of that decision had to do with the school system there and the suitability of the right place to raise a family. We ended up settling in a small community that I live in now, called Bainbridge Island, Washington. It has an amazing community spirit which we decided was a great place for kids to grow up. It is a very safe place with great schools. It is one of those places where you did not think you could raise kids like this in the United States anymore. It was almost like being back in the 70s.

I moved up to Bainbridge Island without a job. I took work where I could find it. I was a project manager for a painting contractor. I was also a bartender. But one thing that I could not get out of my head was that I wanted to do something for myself. I did not want to work for someone else. So I ended up going into business for myself, based on my background experiences in EMS. I started up 2 businesses in a span of 3 years that were based on emergency medicine, around training, and education. While I found these businesses rewarding, I could not figure out how to make a living from them. So, I closed those businesses down.

Then I went into the manufacturing business. Since I was an avid motorcycle rider, I saw that there was a gap in the market, so I invented a product to take to market. I did this for 2 to 3 years. I found that all my businesses were successful, to a point. I could not figure out what was between me and true success.

In addition, I really wasn't happy with my businesses. The only person that had to be responsible for my businesses was me. When I got to thinking about it, I realized that the only thing that they had in common, was me.

So I reached out to a friend of mine and she referred me to a coach. So that is when I hired my first coach. This was maybe back in 2009 or 2010. I was associated with this coach for a year and a half. Coaching had a profound impact on me. The language and the work was really familiar to me, because it was the type of work that I had done with Landmark Education, way back when I was 16 years old. But it had its own specific direction with it that really resonated with me and was a welcoming place. It shifted both my effectiveness like my productivity and what I got done. At the same time, it made a huge impact on the way I felt about my business, which was kind of like "mind blowing."

Before I knew it, I found myself more interested in a conversation about coaching and how it made a difference in myself, in others, and maybe even where it might make a difference in the world, than I was about my business. When I discovered that, I brought it to the attention of my coach and told them that this was what was going on. They said, great, but what is there to do about that? I said that I think that I actually need to become a coach. And so in 2011, I made a commitment and I jumped into a yearlong coach training program.

At the time, though, I wasn't really exactly sure that I wanted to become a coach. I knew that I just wanted to be part of the training and to be part of what there was to see. But by the time that I was done with the program, I became convinced that I wanted to become a coach. I ended up selling my businesses and my last investment that I had in my business and started my coaching career at that time. I have been coaching now, in 2016, for about 5 years.

Nobody arrives, there is no arrival, there is no dollar figure, there is no inner peace, there is no perfection, there is no it's done, when it comes to developing yourself. There is always a process. Your life is either expanding or contracting. It is never static. Most people let their lives contract and get smaller and smaller as a way to protect themselves, or control their lives, as opposed to being challenged to get outside of their comfort zone.

That has probably been the biggest gift of this work. If no one arrives, then there's no place to go. If you think about happiness and contentment, joy and wholeness are when you lose that weight, or make that money, or have that relationship, you will discover that the bad news is when you get there, and it is just more of the same. So really, you are just as "there" right now as you will ever be. There is no getting there, there is only the here and now. That brings some focus, some urgency, and a huge amount of possibility that otherwise would not exist for people.

You get to be both the author and beneficiary of your experience and prospective on life. You get the say over everything in your life. It really doesn't matter what circumstances change around you. People are going to be born and people will die. Money is going to come and money is going to go. Relationships will come and go. People will grow up and go on with their lives. People who have been around you for a long time will finally leave you sometime in your life. That is just the way nature is in life.

This work is a continual gift for me. I have found myself in a place where I can see a lifetime's worth of insight in my work. I am really grateful for this work and what it can bring to both myself and others. Sharing my life's experiences and what I am passionate about in life, because the only thing that I can speak with authority on, are my own experiences, and nothing more. Everything beyond this is just opinions. Actually, I don't think that a day goes by, that I don't try to share myself, or provide a reflection to make a difference for others. The idea that there is a "right" way to do anything is a joke. I don't think that there is a right way to live this life, the right way to get something done. I think that we are given "gifts" that enable us to follow a unique path that can only be our own. We can get a reflection of other people's struggles, their insights, or what they have learned about themselves or others.

**Gill Holland**
**Business Field:** Medical Doctor
**Business Name:** Ocotillo Family Medicine
**Current Position:** Chandler Regional Hospital - Family Physician

## Personal Background:

I was born and raised in El Paso, Texas. I lived there until I was 18 years old. My family includes 2 siblings, a younger brother, and younger sister. I went to Coronado High School in El Paso. I then graduated from the University of Texas, at Austin with a Biology degree. I went on to medical school at the Medical College of Wisconsin.

As far as sports activities in high school and college, I did not participate. I was always athletically challenged. In my youth, I was always lucky to weigh in around 120 pounds. For many years I was always very thin.

At an early age I became interested in music. I started playing the piano at age 9. Then I started writing music in my early teens. I found a book at the El Paso Library on music and copyrighting. At the age of 15, I was writing and copyrighting my own music. Back then, since there was no internet, it was a little more difficult to figure out how to compose, write, etc.

While in college, even though my major was Biology, I took some courses in music. While I was in medical school, I had a voice coach for a couple of years. I did this to keep me sane and balanced while studying medicine. I felt that the rigorous curriculum of medicine and science could best be offset by my music, allowing me to maintain a human element to my persona.

I always wanted to become a doctor because I thought that I could make a difference helping people. From the age of 3, I used to say that I was going to grow up and become a doctor. I thought that if I could become a doctor, maybe the kids in the future would not need to get shots. Of course that did not happen, but that was a great idea to have, and illustrates my desire to help others, which was a part of me at an early age, and much before I had an opportunity to mature into adulthood.

I did OK on my grades in high school and college. I had to work hard because the grades did not come easy, as with some other students. Like I said, I worked hard and I was also pretty lucky. Some people graduated summa cum laude, I graduated, "Thank You Lord!" Just because I did not graduate #1 in my class, did not mean that I could not be a good or great doctor. I graduated from medical school in 2000.

After graduating from medical school, I moved to Phoenix for my residency. I completed my residency at St. Josephs' Hospital. Initially I wanted to be a pediatrician and that is why I went to the Medical College of Wisconsin. There was a professor at MCW who was world renowned in the field of pediatrics. While in medical school, I learned that adults were not that bad or as scary as I originally thought. I wanted to do something where I was at the interface of medicine and patients. "At the door of medicine," so to speak. I was trying to determine where I could make the most impact in helping people. Whether it was adults or children. I found out that once you get patients at a specialty level, the diagnosis is already made, there is little detective work. The patient has already been "teed up" and ready to go for you.

So towards the end of medical school I kept thinking, "What specialty am I going to pick?" I then started thinking about emergency medicine or Family Medicine. I flipped a coin and it landed on "tails." That is how I made my decision on Family Medicine.

Right after my residency, I became a free-lance medical reporter for CNN Español. I speak Spanish fluently, and I used those skills on the local TV station *Mas Arizona*, as their medical correspondent.

I really don't know how you would measure the success of my endeavor in this position. I think as long as you are happy and you have made a difference, then you have met the definition of success. In medical reporting you are trying to educate the masses. You are also trying to keep whichever entities that are keeping you on the air, happy as well. So you have to be doing a good job for your "patients and sponsors," so to speak. It is kind of a juggling act to make everyone involved, satisfied.

My parents had a positive impact in every success that I have had in my life. They have always been there for me. They have been a rock whenever I have had self-doubts or needed direction, I could always go to them. They may not always have had the right answers, but they at least tried, and that part is invaluable. Neither one of my parents graduated from high school. They are both from Mexico. My dad came to the states over 50 years ago. When he got here, he opened up a small clothing shop in El Paso. My mom came to the states about 40 years ago. She met my dad on vacation and dated for a couple of weeks and were married in a few months. Now that is what I call a real success story!

I was doing medical correspondent work as a resident. When I finished my residency, I was also working for Urgent Care for a year. All the while I was trying to decide if the next step was going to be in medical journalism or open a medical practice. My wife at the time and I discussed this, and she thought that it might be better to open up a medical practice. So I stayed away from the journalism. So, that was the route that I took as we chose it together.

I opened my practice in 2003. Over the years, I have employed a naturopathic physician and a physician assistant. Nurse practitioners and physician assistants can both write prescriptions. Right now the rules are a nurse practitioner can "open up a shop" on their own, whereas a physician's assistant can't. As far as which is better, it boils down to the specific individual. Some are great; some are not - the same as physicians.

Later, I merged the practice with a larger entity because of the rising cost of running a practice, along with the difficulty of keeping up with the process of getting paid and keeping the doors open. Finances can be an absolute killer.

Having to find ways to keep the money stream coming in, making sure that your billing people are doing the right things, and the old nemesis of costs that keep going up, with your revenues that keep going down, the demands on a practice that keep getting greater as time moves forward in your practice. Unfortunately, it is an economy of scale. The larger your practice, the easier it is to facilitate the costs and revenues. Most single practices in the country today are failing or have failed. We have gone from over 60% of physicians being in private practice, to fewer than 30%, in just a few years.

It was not just the Affordable Care Act that had a negative impact on these types of practices. It can't be singled out as just that. It is every step of the way where you have government involvement that has changed the rules of the game. The more work that goes into a practice that is unpaid for, the more difficult it becomes for the physician to run the business and sustain it. The more individuals involved in the process taking a salary, the more expensive the process will become.

When we talk about people being successful, even as a physician, I really don't see myself as a success. I see myself as doing the right thing and caring about people. As long as I do my best and to help someone, then I am living the right life.

At this time in my life, things are changing rapidly. My vision for my medical future is to take a good look at the many types of solicitations that I have received as a physician. As for being in primary care, administrative medicine, or wound medicine, I really don't know. What I am trying to do is weigh a quality of life, with being able to find a way to be able to spend more time with my children and loved ones.

It is funny when you talk about success. I feel like in many ways I have not been successful. I was divorced after opening up my medical practice. It was unfortunate that I had to leave the situation. I left when my kids were very young at the time. They were 2 and 4, and I lost out on a family. I think the real success is when you can have the family and the practice both. I think that Shakespeare said in his dying days that, "The most important thing is family." I agree.

Every patient is someone's family member. If I can remember that everyone is someone's father, mother, brother or sister, child, relative, loved one etc., and then my eye is on what is important. Even a 90 year person is someone's child. They are all human and that is what keeps me engaged as well as keeping my "eye on the ball." As happens in medicine, a lot of people burn out, and they just see the patient in room #3 as the "gall bladder," not as Mr. Jones' wife, mother or grandmother.

In another area, I have always been playing music, and have kept up with my writing of music. In the past few years, actually a patient at the practice was into music and the music industry. As we started talking about music, he asked me why I was not pursuing a musical career. Then I thought to myself, yeah, why am I not doing it? So, I started doing a little bit more with my writing of music, and actually tried to put it out there. I am not really good at performing and getting up on a stage in front of a lot of people. I do not like to sing in front of people. But, I figured that I had better start doing it, if I ever had a chance for any kind of success in the music business. I am a composer, I play piano and recently learned how to play guitar, as well as arrange and compose music.

I have met with some limited success and recognition. I have also been getting some attention from some of the people in the industry. A while back, *Phoenix Magazine* reached out to me because they had heard, through different channels, about what I was doing. Then they became interested. I really do not have an idea of where I am going to be going with my music career in the next 2-3 years. I look at my music that same way that I look at medicine.

If I am able to change or touch someone in a positive manner, then I am successful for that person. When a lot of people look at someone being successful, they sometimes look at how much money a person makes, or net worth. For me, money comes and goes. Money seems to be the new "idol." People seem to worship it more than good values or friendships.

As far as giving back, that process can take a lot of different forms. I have helped others make recordings and I do that just for fun. I have been to a number of free clinics, both in Phoenix, and down at the border of Nogales, to offer free services. Since I speak fluent Spanish, this has enabled me to be comfortable with the patients and vice-versa.

I have also recently become a "*mohel*," which is the name of the person who performs a bris, the ceremonial religious circumcision for a Jewish boy once he turns 8 days old. It was a way that I could offer something back to the Jewish community. When a baby boy is 8 days old, they get their Jewish name and are welcomed into the Jewish community. This is something that I started to do, because I remembered when my son was born, it was very difficult to find someone to perform his procedure.

There is a need in the Phoenix area, so I went to get special training to do it. There is a fee for the service, but I in turn give this money back to a charity. This has traditionally been done for the last 3,500 years. The younger generation is doing this as well. What I think has happened, is that there are a lot less people who want to perform this, because of the liability issue. Also, it is not very lucrative financially. If people think that they can do it to make money, it is not going to be beneficial for them. They think that it takes too much time away from their jobs. But to me, if it is important to me, then I will take the time to do it.

**Greg DePaola**
**Business Field:** GM Car Sales
**Business Name:** Coulter Motor Company
**Current Position:** Executive Manager

**Personal Background**

I was born in October of 1960, in Winchester, Massachusetts, and lived there for 5 years. My parents are Dan & Phyllis Connors. My mom and I left my father when I was 1 year old. My mom's sister helped raise me until I was three and one-half years old.

My biological father and I had no relationship. In fact, he and I have had only 1 conversation since June of 1986. On the day before my marriage to my first wife, he called to congratulate me, and I haven't heard from him since.

My mom met a man named Tom. He adopted me when I was 5 years old, and he's been the only dad I've ever known. Because of this, I always refer to him as my dad, and will do so throughout this profile.

At five and one-half years old, we moved to the Cape, and Dad and Mom started an accounting firm. Dad was the CPA and Mom was the secretary. They began this home-based business with only one asset - a calculator, and only 1 client - a builder on the Cape. In time, the business grew to a firm with 20 employees, and was one of the largest firms on the Cape.

Dad always had a plan for me and he always pushed me to accomplish things. He and Mom encouraged me with school and work. But for them, I would not be who I am today. Mom and Dad divorced when I was 20, and it had a profound, negative impact on my life. Though dad and I parted, we still communicated. He died when he was 67 (I was then 44). I still thank him for his lessons: Live with integrity; declare your plans and intentions out loud; and then go achieve them. Knowing my interest in cars and the car business, he once said, "If you are going to get into the car business, don't be a 'car guy'. Instead, be a businessman in the car business." I'll never forget him.

As a result of my issues at school, and following my parents' divorce, I lived through some bad times. Things got so bad that my dad disowned me and my mom threw me out of her house. I landed a lousy job at a local bar as a "Bar Back." I ended up living with a bunch of guys in a house we shared. My "room" was a closet - literally. I slept on a thin mattress on the floor of this closet! After 8 months, my mom was able to locate me through my work, and she sat down with me - in this closet. She expressed her disapproval in no uncertain terms, and declared that I had to make a decision - either continue to live this lousy life, or make a better life for myself. She invited me back home.

When you work in the car business, it can be really hard to balance one's business life and personal life. We spend an extraordinary amount of time on the showroom floor, in the service bays, and just talking with customers and prospects. All this time away from home comes at no cost to me, thanks to my current wife, Robin. She is one of the primary reasons for my success. She handles everything - and I mean EVERYTHING - outside of my work. She deals with bills, shopping, clothes, etc.

She provided me the freedom I need in order to do what needs to be done. It is my job to build and grow a strong dealership here in the Southeast Valley, and it's her job to fill in the rest. For example, we recently experienced an air conditioning problem at our house. Did I have to address the issue? No! Robin solicited competitive quotes and discerned what each contractor was offering by way of tonnage and SEER ratings. Without her help, I would have been hard pressed to spend the time needed to gather all this information. I am very, very fortunate to have Robin as an equal partner at my side.

**School**

School was always a challenge for me. I consistently got poor grades, despite being considered by most people to be very bright. Mom and Dad first tried to help by sending me to a private school called The Tabor Academy in Marion, Massachusetts. Tabor was good for me, as they taught me how to learn. With the help of my tutors, I mastered the skill of researching anything I wanted to know. I went there for a couple of years of high school, and then transferred to Barnstable High School for my senior year.

But I still achieved only mediocre grades. Finally, my parents sent me to Massachusetts General Hospital for testing. We learned that I had dyslexia and a condition referred to as "Test Block." People with this condition simply freeze up when presented with a test. It was recommended that I see a psychologist. Instead, my dad enrolled me in The American International College (AIC) in Springfield, Massachusetts. This was a big turning point in my life. AIC specializes in educating people who suffer with learning disabilities like mine.

I met a man named Curtis Blake, the founder of Friendly's Ice Cream. He was also one of AIC's largest benefactors. He was dyslexic himself, and gave large donations to AIC to support their work to help people like himself - people like me.

AIC developed a number of programs, one of which was to create audio tapes for blind students. It turned out that I was an audible learner, not a visual learner. The floodgates opened, and my grades immediately skyrocketed. After 2 successful years at AIC, but shy of earning a degree, I decided I had had enough of school.

My dad sat me down and explained that many successful people had no formal degrees. He and others, many of whom were graduates of AIC, shared their stories of success with me, and they all believed in the following principles: Have a strong work ethic, learn and master every facet of the things that interest you, build a foundation of successful acquaintances, be truthful to yourself, and "go with your gut."

### World of Work

As early as Junior High School, I absolutely knew that I was interested in cars. I could recognize their year, make and model, even from a distance. For example, at the age of 15, during a blinding snow storm, I spotted a vehicle, and knew immediately, despite very poor visibility, that it was a Ford Police Cruiser. Another thing I knew for sure - I did not want to work in the fast food service industry. So, while in high school, and with the encouragement of my dad, I started my own valet parking service in partnership with 3 of my high school buddies. The money I made running this little business made it possible for me to start flying lessons at age 16, and earn my pilot's license by the time I was 17!

As you read above, my life was not that great for a while. By the time 1980 rolled around, I had a grand total of $100 to my name, and was driving a "luxurious" 1973 light blue Ford Fairmont. Then things started to turn around. I happened to meet the New Truck Manager, the General Manager, and the Owner of a car dealership located in Boston. They were in town for a GM Truck Meeting. During our brief conversation, they told me I would make a great car salesman. They said it would be my niche in life - and they were right.

I then drove from Cape Cod to Boston and applied for a job at Clay Chevrolet. Paul Stratford, the General Manager of that store, became my mentor for the next 8 years of my new life. I spent my first 3 years there as a salesperson, and the next 5 as the Used Vehicle Manager!

I then attended my brother's wedding. He married a woman in Denver who owned a top-of-the-line women's apparel store. At the wedding reception, I was seated next to "Chuck," a man who owned 8 dealerships in the Denver area. We discussed my career and my experience in the car business. He convinced me and my wife at that time to move to Denver to work for him. My first position with him was as his New Car Manager. Eighteen months later, in 1993, I was promoted to become his General Sales Manager - a position I held for 3 years. Following this run, I moved to Arizona and took a position as the General Sales Manager of Thorobred Chevrolet.

From 1999 to 2003, I ran a Chevrolet store in Mesa, Arizona, owned by "Mitch." He was "the bomb" to work for. In fact, working for him was like going to "Harvard" for car sales and salesmanship techniques. Despite my years of experience, I learned so much from Mitch, and my skill set advanced to the next level.

Next, I was recruited to join a 14-store organization back in Denver. I began as the Used Car Director, but quickly rose to the position of Director of Operations for the entire organization. This experience lasted from 2003 to 2007. Near its end, I decided that I wanted to return to Arizona.

I had previously met a man named Bill Coulter. I called him expressing my interest in joining his 4-store automobile sales organization. In January of 2008, Bill called to say that we should meet. I flew to Phoenix and told him I wanted to run one of his "Big Box" stores. He said that if I could improve the operation of his Infiniti store, he would then promote me to one of his larger stores.

I had my work at the Infiniti store cut out for me. It was not performing to Bill's expectations. I started there in the first week of April, 2008, and worked very, very hard to turn it around, which finally lead to the chance to manage a "Big Box" store.

### Philosophy

As a single salesperson, I made some good money by selling a lot of cars. Some critical lessons I learned early on include:

43

- Find common ground fast
- Always ask open-ended questions
- Listen - REALLY listen
- Mirror the posture of the person you are dealing with
- Use an absolute amount of common sense at all times
- Do what you enjoy and enjoy what you do

A large part of my success in selling cars was due to my knack for "reading" people, and then applying critical sales principles. Another early part of my success was due to the fact that I had grown up and lived in Cape Cod - the home of highly successful people like the DuPonts and the Mellons. My dad was successful in his business and joined a country club. As a result, I had multiple opportunities to meet, speak with, and really listen to a large array of highly successful people.

In mentoring my own employees, I work to impress upon them the need to set up first class processes, and to establish procedures that support and advance those processes. For example, I tell them to set up their departments for what I call "management by sight." For instance, organize your vehicles into separate areas - vehicles just unloaded by the transport truck go here, vehicles waiting to be serviced go over there, and vehicles prepped for delivery go somewhere else. This way, you know exactly how many cars are in each area, and you can manage them by sight. As you look the areas over, you can see what's in and out of control. You don't have to communicate with anyone since you can literally see what is right and wrong with the store.

I have been fortunate with recruiting "good to great" personnel over the years. Let's face it, if you have enough money, sooner or later, you can probably just buy a dealership. But running a store on a day to day, week to week, and month to month basis requires good, but also great, personnel who are in it for the long haul. The book, <u>Good to Great</u>, by Jim Collins, taught me a lot about how to move yourself and others from being just good, to accelerate to a higher level. It also taught me how to continually challenge myself as well as others around me.

Remember, you are building a foundation for your business. If the footer on which you lay your cement blocks is poor, the house will not be level. In time, it may not even be erect! It is the same with people. Invest in them just as you would invest in technology. As you build your business, it is important to recognize the personnel who have vision, and who can direct activities around them. Two quick stories serve as illustrations:

### The Story of Mark

Mark was a Lot Attendant and ran my Pre-Delivery Inspection process. I had a neighbor who was having an issue with the garage door opener feature in his vehicle. Mark went to his house, knocked on the door, introduced himself as a representative of my store, and fixed the problem. I promptly received feedback from my neighbor that Mark was one of the most courteous, professional, and responsible service persons he had seen in a long time. This intrigued me. I asked Mark, "What are you doing as a lot attendant?" Even though he replied that he felt he was doing just fine as a lot attendant, I saw in him something more. I asked him to think about managing people (not just things). He agreed to give it a try. I promoted him to the position of Internal Service Writer - a position in which he would handle the majority of service problems and all in-house service activities. When he was the "garage door opener fixer" he made $8.25 per hour. He now makes $42K per year, but has the potential to increase that income to $50K to $100K+ per year. He has become my "go-to guy," and his new responsibilities have made a world of difference to him and his family. This is an example of getting the right person in the right seat on your bus.

### The Story of Michael

Michael was a kid who came into the Infiniti store to apply for a job as a receptionist. I asked, "Is that all you want?" He said, "Yes, it is." A few months later, I and others noticed that he was a "whiz bang" on computers. He was also like a sponge at picking up information by listening, and then applying what he learned. He is now my Warranty Clerk, and tracks all information to and from our store to the manufacturer for our Infiniti location.

Tip: Go out and recruit the best possible personnel based upon the criteria you establish for positions. Experience is not always my top priority. I look for someone who can devise and maintain the processes and procedures that make a store successful. Selecting the right people at the right time is critical in any business.

The art of listening seems to have become a lost art. While there are many things that need to be done if an Executive Manager intends to maintain and grow the store's profit position, I think it all begins with effective listening. Listening to the lot attendant, the sales manager, the receptionist, the customer, and anyone and everyone else who has an association with your store, will, when done correctly, yield tremendous insight into what's right and wrong with an organization. And while I'm at it, let me add that paying attention to small details can make a big difference. For example, many stores don't place much emphasis on the role of the receptionist. But I ask you, who is the first person customers and others meet when they walk into a dealership? He or she is the store's first opportunity to make a great impression. It pays to pay attention to this very important position!

The Coulter Family has been in business in the Greater Metro Phoenix Area going on 100 years. An essential element of that long and successful history is the need to take care of our customers. Achieving the highest levels of Customer Satisfaction is a key component of my duties to Mr. Coulter. Once you've worked hard to earn a customer's business, maintaining high customer satisfaction keeps sales and service going. My goal is to instill this attitude into the minds and practices of all of my employees. Three short stories will serve to illustrate this:

### Q-56
One day, at around 9:00 a.m., as I walked through the Infiniti store, I noticed a blue Q-56

parked in the Service Drive. The tailgate was propped open with a broomstick. I asked the Service Manager about it, and learned that we were waiting for authorization from Infiniti to make the repair. At 2:00, I noticed 2 women. I spoke to them and learned that the Q-56 belonged to one of them. We still had no Infiniti authorization, and I let them know this. As we chatted, I also learned that this lady's husband was serving in Iraq as a pilot for a Special Forces unit. I immediately authorized the $1100 repair, and advised her that we would not only take care of it, but would also give her a free loaner vehicle to use while we performed the work. They both broke into tears - tears of joy. Three months later, the wife and her husband came into the store. Her husband, the pilot, gave me a big box. It contained a letter of appreciation, a US flag and a letter of authenticity. Apparently, the Coulter Infiniti story was now well known to many service personnel in Iraq, and in appreciation, his unit flew a special mission, called Python 40, in honor of Coulter Infiniti.

### Vets Cars

At Coulter Cadillac, Buick & GMC in Tempe, Arizona - my current store - I enrolled us in the Vets Cars Program. Under it, we commit to providing the highest levels of sales, service and integrity to our nation's active and former Military Service Men and Women, and their families. We appreciate their sacrifices, and honor it, not only with expressions of gratitude, but also with special pricing and special treatment. We see it as the least we can do for the valiant warriors who strive to protect us and our freedoms.

**Folds of Honor**

At our Tempe Cadillac, Buick & GMC store, we also participate in the Folds of Honor Program. Under it, a folded flag is given to the families of each of "The Fallen." The program works to address the needs of over a million dependents - people who are adversely affected by deployments. For instance, because more than 75% of our service men and women do not qualify for financial scholarship assistance, Folds of Honor provides educational scholarships to the families of members of the military who have been disabled, or worse, killed in action. Since 2007, over 7000 scholarships have been awarded. Coulter is proud to be a part of this important program, and will continue to support it - financially and otherwise.

As you can see, giving back - to our customers, to the military, and to their families - is an important part of the culture I work hard to create and foster in my store. I train all my salespeople to treat all our customers with respect, and to honor them by: Being up front; Doing the right thing; Staying involved – even after the sale; and NEVER lying or even bending the truth. Paradoxically, it is my experience that the more you give, the more you receive in return.

**Conclusions**

Despite learning disabilities, despite setbacks, despite life decision mistakes, success is still possible, but only with the help, guidance and support of others. Course corrections are always an option, and can lead to life-changing results. The advice given to me by others - the advice that I've mentioned in this profile - will work for anyone. At my current stage in life, I am now in a position to offer to others the kinds of help, guidance and support that I was given. Perhaps, one day, someone else might mention their experiences with me in their own profile, just as I've included others in my own.

**Joseph Simon Pongratz**
**Business Field:** Orthotics and Prosthetics, Medical Device Innovation, & Real Estate
**Business Names:** Pongratz Orthotics and Prosthetics, Inc., CureVentions, A and J Pongratz, LLC and JSP, LLC
**Business Position:** POP - President - Clinical Director, CV-CEO Medical, Device Innovation, A and J Pongratz, LLC - Residential Real Estate Management, JSP, LLC - Commercial Real Estate Management

**Personal Background:**

I am of Hungarian, German, and Polish heritage. My parents are Andrew Tibor Pongratz and Carolyn Buba Pongratz. My father, Andrew is 78 years old, has been involved in real estate, has been a life insurance broker, and today he enjoys traveling with Hungarian musical tour groups.

My mother, Carolyn is 72 years old and has spent her entire life as a music director at various Catholic Churches in Boston and here in Arizona. When she retired from that career, she started teaching religious education. She is also a full-time "Grammy" to many (17 and counting) grandchildren.

My father is of European descent and carries many old fashioned attributes with his personality. He and his family (9 brothers and sisters) escaped from the Hungarian Revolution when Soviet Russia invaded Hungary in 1956. They settled in the eastern United States and began rebuilding their lives as immigrants here in the US. He is a free speaker with his thoughts and words. He is very thankful for the life he has worked so hard for and he is still very proud of his Hungarian heritage.

My father is a smart businessman who drives his personality as a conservative spender/thinker and decision maker. This mindset was the strength of my father, as he grew up searching for various occupations to support our family of 5 kids. My dad grew up in a different era and mindset.

I always remember my dad being involved in many disciplines of work, including selling real estate, insurance, and travel agencies. Whatever his occupation, he was always around. He did not go to an office. He was there for us at home and for our dinner, as his work was mostly from a "home" office. When I woke up in the morning, he was there. When I came home at night, he was there. He was available to drive us to soccer practice.

My mother, being one of 2 girls, was the youngest in her family. She was raised with Polish-German traits by stern parents in a small town outside of Boston. My mother's personality is very tender, generous, and always caring. She made sure each of her kids had every necessity growing up with clothes, shoes, and great food! She was many years younger than her sister and grew up as the little one.

She followed her sister's footsteps as a musician and an accomplished music director. She continued to do this as we moved from Boston to Arizona in 1979. It seemed my father worked to pay the bigger bills and my mother worked to help and clothe the family. We did not meet our grandfather on my dad's side and were very young when Grandma Pongratz passed.

We loved growing up with my mother's parents named "Grampy" and "Gammy." Going over for Polish Kielbasa and soups was always a treat. Also, my mom's sister married my dad's brother. We were always together for all of the Christmas and Easter holidays. My mom was home too. Even though she may have been occupied with the church music or concerts, she was home for a "Sunday" family dinner at our house every night!

My parent's relationship growing up was strong, faith based, an example of getting through tough times, and now is all about living their legacy. I remember our home was filled with the typical chaos from 5 kids and my parents handled each event in stride. Their communication was quiet and usually discussed the day's events and the next too. We grew up with my dad's traveling desires, touring the USA in our motor home each summer.

Today, each family gathering is another opportunity for them to enjoy, smile, and reflect back to the days we were all growing up. They are sure to add a proud story about one of us 5 kids doing something that stirred their memory. My parents are still affectionate today toward each other. It's not uncommon for them to take romantic trips to celebrate life, or to see them holding hands during a walk, or while sitting in church.

Growing up in a house with 5 kids, there was plenty of disciplining needed. My 3 brothers and I were involved in something every day that usually got us time-out in our rooms, or sitting in a corner. We were not spanked by my mother, but we were by my father. My dad was not a big man so I remember he would use his hands or a belt. I do remember that my dad had a very direct voice. You knew when he was mad and when you were in trouble. Usually by that point we stopped what we were doing and my dad did not have to spank us.

Disciplining our kids today is different than when I was growing up. I remember getting a lot of the strict European-German yelling at us, then a spanking. Today we are more about removing privileges, discussing the wrong behavior, having our kids think about what they did wrong, and what the correct behavior is. We do time-outs and we apologize for behavior issues.

My parents were both raised in a "you do what you have to do world." Although I did not spend many moments with them during discussions and major issues, we seemed to always get through major issues. One major issue for our family was relocating to Arizona when I was 9 years old, for my dad's job opportunity.

My parents wanted to move. However, all our family was in Boston so the decision was difficult, and we did what we had to do. Today, I see that my parents always reflect back to the "back in our day this is what we would have done," when discussing major issues.

I had a great relationship with my parents growing up. My mom and I would attend church together every Sunday as I played guitar in the choir that she directed. On weekends, I assisted setting up the music sound system with my mom on Saturday and Sundays. My mom is wonderfully caring and always as generous as one can be.

I related to my mom very well growing up, because she was very nurturing and easy to communicate with. My father was the one who always kept us going and he was the determined one. He was there for every soccer practice and football game transporting my brothers and me.

I speak to my parents weekly about various things going on in our ever-changing family. They are very involved with our kids wanting to come see sporting events and coming for dinners. They seem to not be slowing down and relaxing these days, because they just returned from another European vacation, and are soon to be going to Minnesota to visit my sister and her family. It is very common for our family to connect many times weekly and discuss the current week's events.

My oldest brother Andy has a very caring and nurturing personality. He will let nothing stand in the way of his 3 kids and his family experiencing *all* life has to offer. He is a hard worker and carries on a family real estate business. His wife Andrea is from Hungary and moved here to spend her life with my brother Andy and start a family in the USA. They have 3 kids who speak Hungarian, all excel in school, and are involved in church, arts, and sports.

My sister is an attorney and was the successful sibling in the family, growing up with perfect grades, and activities to follow. "The Rose among the Thorns" we called her. She was a very good example of an older sister to have during our high school days, when we started dating and building relationships. She made sure we maintained our morals, discipline, and respect for all people. She kept an eye on her brothers. Teri was the first sibling to marry her husband named Charlie. Charlie comes from a very strong German family who grew up in

Minnesota. He has a very caring personality and is full of adventure. Teri and Charlie have 4 kids and live in Minnesota.

My middle brother Ed was a fun learning experience for me growing up. He has a "Rock Star" personality who is always pushing the "fun" limits. Ed has a successful construction business which he manages with his wife Stacie. Stacie brings a perfect blend of rock star wife and calmness to their lives. She has her hands full as a health care case manager, following Ed and his life adventures, and raising their 2 boys who are very accomplished soccer players and fine young boys.

My younger brother Steve is a very analytical thinker and takes his time with decisions. He is organized and scheduled to meet the responsibilities in his life with his wife Serrina, his 2 kids, and 1 step-son. Steve is the youngest and was raised as the caboose in the family train, meaning he had plenty of, examples to learn from. He was a very smart thinker and planner. He was also a very accomplished soccer player, leading his high school and other teams to many championships. Steve is a business manager and runs a sporting distribution business, along with following and coaching his son's baseball teams. This is a true passion of his. Steve is a very active family man and father.

My siblings and I were all very close growing up. I was closest with my two brothers, Ed and Steve. The 3 of us were very close in age, playing sports, all activities like Cub Scouts, and even religious education. We supported each other, protected each other, and cared for each other. Our parents raised us to not fight, not to be against each other, but to respect and care for each other. We did the best we could, but of course, as brothers, there were many battles on and off the field of sports and life. All of our siblings spent a lot of time together at home, on sports fields, and growing up attending the same school.

Today, it is not uncommon to spend several days a week visiting siblings who mostly live here in Arizona. Two of my brothers, Ed and Steve, live very close. We often watch sporting events together, attend concerts, or just stop by and have lunch. My eldest brother Andy lives in Tucson. We see him during family events. Once in a while, we also have lunch in Tucson while I am there for business. We communicate with our sister Teri, who lives in Minnesota through phone calls or email. Her family has made a few trips a year to Arizona with her 4 kids to visit for many different family gatherings

My childhood was very positive in relation to my family, friends and school experiences. The memories I have that are closest to me, are sharing all these experiences with my brothers and sister, who were always part of my childhood.

All 5 siblings are very close in age, so we shared schools, sporting teams, friends, and everything having to do with growing up together. We supported, looked out for, and protected each other in every activity we were involved in. Almost every season of playing soccer, baseball or football was with one of my brothers.

My favorite childhood memory is having my brothers next to me, supporting me, pushing me, and racing me, while we laughed and enjoyed every minute growing up. I don't think I have a negative childhood memory.

My high school years were the best years for me. Every semester, I was involved in some type of activity, including football, soccer, track, and student council. Out of school I was very active in our church choir and Fellowship of Christian Athletes. My high school sport teams were top rated and mostly undefeated. This allowed young students to learn responsibility, respect, team involvement and *discipline*. All these characteristics proved to be crucial to be "successful" in life.

I would also add that the "Best Friends" I had in high school, are still my best friends today. I am very thankful for those past memories and ongoing lifelong memories. I would say my favorite activities were sports. Then I became interested in prosthetics and orthotics, when I was exposed to Health Related Occupations. I would have to say that these years molded me and provided guidance allowing me to accomplish where I am today.

My concerns growing up were minimal. I had a fantastic family, was involved in very successful sporting teams, and had a great job. My jobs were in orthotics and prosthetic businesses and provided above average wages for a high school student. But most importantly, they provided a great foundation for my future profession. There was really nothing that I was worried about, because I knew my dreams were very close, and I had a great foundation to get there.

Early on I learned not to "cheat" to win. My brothers and I were competitive and we were good athletes with great sportsmanship. As the 4th child in our family, I remember I was not the fastest kid when I was young. I remember growing up, while in my early teens, something clicked, and I noticed I was the fastest kid on the playground. From my brothers, I was lucky to learn competition is a very good quality, used in the right frame of mind.

Our family was not rich, but Mom and Dad always made sure we had what we needed. Our upbringing was focused more on a humble, non-extravagant lifestyle as my parents raised us how they were raised, very conservative. My dad, from European upbringing, where the communists didn't allow anyone to have items of wealth, and my mom, who was raised with strict German Polish traits in Randolph, Massachusetts, a small town outside Boston.

When we moved to Arizona, I remember having good friends who used to let me have their "Vans" shoes, when they were done with them. I thought those shoes were terrible, I liked the ones my mom bought me much better. There was a value to being raised humble, as it gives you a perspective to respect and value everything, and treasure the small things in life. Reflecting back, I recall a story of my dad having only 10 cents in his pocket. Our family had a continued value for family gatherings with meals and family gatherings.

Growing up, my parents showed family support. They were there for everything: football games in the freezing rain, soccer games all over the state, and track meets in the 110 degree sun. They were very supportive with literally anything all of us kids needed. My brothers and sister were also there and supported all the activities we shared. I mostly enjoyed coming home Friday nights after football games and my parents were still awake and asked me all kinds of questions about the game and the key plays. They were new to football, so they had many questions. It was obvious my parents enjoyed watching all of us kids excel in all aspects of life, including sports and extracurricular activities.

We lived in Boston, Massachusetts during most of my childhood years where both my father's and mother's siblings lived as well. I have close to 50 cousins who we grew up and we interacted with very often around Boston. What great memories I have of my extended family. We were very close in age growing up, allowing us to develop strong friendships.

Then in 1979 we moved to Arizona, where there was no other family or cousins living. This was somewhat of a family shock. We were used to all families being together for every event and holiday like Christmas and the 4th of July. Over the years, many of us still maintain contact and have vacationed together, and visited each other's homes and families. Still today, we continue a yearly cousins hunting trip here in Arizona.

Education was very important in our family. As far as my educational background, I attended Amphitheater High School, Tucson, Arizona and graduated in 1988. Next I enrolled at the University of Arizona, Tucson, Arizona in 1988. In 1992, I received a degree BS BioMechanics.

I continued with postgraduate school at Northwestern University Prosthetic Orthotic Center, in Chicago from 1992-1993. I received a Certificate in Prosthetics and Orthotics. I then became a

Certified Prosthetics Orthoptist in 1996 - American Board for Certification Orthotics and Prosthetics, followed by a Fellow American Academy Orthotics and Prosthetics (FAAOP) in 1999.

Further education included a residency at De La Torre O&P, in Pittsburgh, Pennsylvania. During the years of 1993-1995, I worked as a Clinical Associate. I worked for 2-3 other companies here in Arizona, before I started my own business, Pongratz Orthotics and Prosthetics (POP) in 1997.

I am currently the president and director of clinical services at Pongratz O&P. The business has grown to have 4 offices here in Arizona with over 25 employees. My role is to oversee the business and assure care is maintained as the industry changes, but our products and service do not. I enjoy having a number of patients. I continue to care for these patients through years of relationships.

I am very satisfied with this career that I have chosen. It certainly allows one to be very creative in manufacturing prosthetic and orthotic devices, while servicing the needs of many people. If there was anything I would be dissatisfied with today, it would be the issues with managed health care, and the loss of benefits our patients deal with on a daily basis. The world of medical care and insurance will forever be changing. I am sorry to see when it changes to decrease the level of benefits for "needing" patients.

My future goals are to maintain the business that I have been running for 19 years. I have also enjoyed developing medical devices which have allowed me to form another company, called CureVentions. This company creates intentional products to promote health and healing. We are currently a global provider of a handful of products. I also enjoy residential and commercial real estate, which my wife Anissa and I do together. We own and manage our own real estate holding company, A and J Pongratz, LLC.

In my spare time I enjoy family gatherings at home, playing with the kids in the yard, playing sports, and playing the guitar in my church music group. My music and my family keep me faith based, which is part of my core values. My mom was instrumental in keeping us kids interested in our faith early on, by introducing me to music, and having the discipline to stick to it.

Our family was started by my meeting my wife Anissa. We met at St Joe's Hospital in Phoenix, Arizona. During that time Anissa was a physical therapist working at St Joe's and I a provider of orthotic and prosthetic services to her rehab team for many years. I would estimate that I had my eye on her for 1-2 years before I even sat down to chat with her. I remember asking her to attend a gathering in February 2003, that many of our mutual friends were attending, and she agreed. I spent the entire event with Anissa chatting about the many similarities in our lives.

In no time at all we were both completely drawn in by our values and similarities we shared: health care professionals, Catholic, strong family values, large families, love of sports, outdoors, and animals...and we were both single! We spent the next several months exploring all these similarities by attending church together, ski trips, going on hikes, yoga, kick boxing, roller blading, and even a family dinner where I sat next to her mom. Yikes!

Mama Felix was awesome! There was no doubt in my mind, I knew Anissa was my life partner. Although I was sure, within weeks we grew our relationship stronger allowing an 8 month "courting" before our engagement in September 2003. Then came our marriage June 2004.

I was attracted to Anissa for many reasons. First, she is stunningly beautiful! When she walks into a room, the atmosphere changes, as though there is a movie star present. As you learn who Anissa is and experience her soft touch, her love, generosity, and an overall spiritual love for all people, you just can't help wanting to be around her forever. Many people very close to me have always expressed how wonderful Anissa is. I always agree and confirm as this is why I married her.

Our relationship has evolved significantly over the years. Obviously there is so much more responsibility in our lives, which has allowed us to concentrate on and observe the most important things in life. For me, I look at Anissa as the person who has created all these blessings with me, and I am so grateful for her. Today I see our relationship with more respect, commitment, responsibility and understanding. Strengths I bring to our marriage; stability, energy, fun, and intimacy. Strengths Anissa brings to our marriage; organization, generosity, love, and tenderness. I would say our foundation and qualities together have created a solid cornerstone for our marriage.

Anissa and I, for the most part, agree on most everything, as we are usually equal thinkers. If we have disagreements, it may be in regards to time management, and how we may book ourselves busy too often. I don't like to have a completely full schedule, but we seem to always have something to do, and somewhere to go.

If we have disagreements, I am usually the one who walks away, if we are mad, and if the topic is getting heated. I am non-confrontational and usually need a few minutes to think some things through. This also allows me to cool off and remember what's important. We usually return to the topic within the day to understand each other's points more clearly. We can then find an understanding and a resolution.

As a couple, we have many strengths in how we get along so well, and have little to complain and argue about. This keeps our home mostly quiet, aside from 5 very loud children, and functioning normally in the day to day activities. We always find time to communicate important issues of the day, week, or month, and plan the next day's schedule together with our kids and businesses. We understand each other's schedules and time commitments. We respect each other's thoughts and opinions.

We both knew, and we both decided together, that we wanted to have a large family. We are also full of more love, energy, and are blessed to be able to provide for our children. This leads into generosity.

We currently have 5 kids, so becoming a parent has had a profound impact on our relationship. I think Anissa and I both understand that there is so much more in life now that we can enjoy together as a family. It's not about us individually anymore; it's about us as a family, with our kids coming first. We have a very tight bond together, knowing how blessed we have been together. And, how much more blessed we are as adoptive parents. Our biological children, Nick age 9, Nate, age 7, and Ava age 5. They have joined us in welcoming their adopted siblings - Anthony and Michael whom are brothers ages 5 & 6. We adopted them on September 10, 2015.

I have to say our children are such beautiful creations who have blessed us. They are lucky to have inherited my wife's beauty and features of darker complexions and olive skin. Nick is the oldest and is in 3$^{rd}$ grade at St Mary Basha Catholic School. He is a great big brother to both of his siblings, protecting and loving them, and he plays with them as much as a big brother can. I always refer to him as our quarterback. Nick is organized, in charge, likes his clothes folded, and he is very sentimental. He will not go anywhere or go to bed without his kisses and hugs. He signs off every night, as we kiss him to bed, saying, "Love you too, see you in the morning, sweet dream, and good night."

Nate is more of a linebacker style of a kid in regards to being crazy, fast, fun, and non-stop. He is 7 and plays equally with Nick, Ava, and his adopted brothers, Anthony and Michael, any time of day. As he grows older, he does love hanging with his "Big" brother, doing big boy stuff with riding quads, sports, Legos, toy cars and riding BMX bikes. He will also play "pretend" with Ava as she cooks and sets up her toy kitchen. Nate is fun about everything he does. I think every family picture we have of Nate, he is either making a funny, loving face, has a toy car in his hand, or is grinning from ear to ear. Nate is also a very loving boy, who likes to cuddle in his favorite pajamas, while watching his favorite cartoons.

Ava is now 5 and soon to be running the family. She has beautiful dark features and is smiling from ear to ear all the time. She loves to play "pretend" with toys, dolls or Dad. She loves to sing, act and dance, and she certainly keeps up with her brothers. Ava is a Daddy's little girl, which I am so in love with. She wants to be in my arms, like she says "all the time." She is the first to call for me in the morning when she wakes. She is the last to say good night, as both Anissa and I read her stories, and tuck her in at night. I can also tell what a special place Ava holds in Anissa's heart as her special little girl. It is so nice seeing Anissa play girl stuff with Ava, as they do their hair, and do dress up fun. Ava is a wonderful daughter with a huge heart, a fun personality who likes to make people laugh, and spread her love as much as she can.

Anissa and I both have strong family cultural backgrounds. We have been raised with the respect to preserve this in our first generation. We personally recognize that knowing where you came from, while preserving this heritage is of utmost importance. We have been discussing ways to preserve this for a child, in regards to lessons in history, country ancestry, and trips to the country.

One of the most important attributes I looked for in a life partner was someone with the strongest values, unprecedented morals, and equal beliefs. We believe in respect of others, taking care of your neighbor, doing the right thing, every time, being generous, and being thankful for *everything* we have been blessed with. Anissa and I have a strong

Catholic faith, which is the foundation of our relationship, and family with high moral standards. We have been raised with and our life mission is to pass these values, morals, and beliefs to our children.

We are blessed to be able to live very comfortably on my income alone. Anissa is the "family manager," handles everything from mom duties like planning the kid's daily activities, their schedules, to volunteering in all the kids' school classrooms. We are blessed that I have a very flexible work schedule with my businesses. I have been able to drive the kids to school or daycare rotating duties with Anissa. I am proud to be able to say I have rarely missed a swim lesson, soccer practice, tee ball, or any other afternoon event. I love being a dad who my kids really know.

My parenting style is really the same as Anissa's, as we learned this together raising our kids. We outwardly love our family and express our emotions openly. Our kids know when we are proud, disappointed, loved, tired, sad, sorry, or excited and ready to play and have fun. I may have different approaches than Anissa when it comes to discipline. She is more of the time out and take away privileges person. I was raised with a stern punishment and spanking. We certainly have our mutual agreements on discipline for our children. We do discuss parenting styles as our kids grow up in this changing world.

Discipline in our home ranges from the timeout, to losing privileges, to being sent to your room. On random occasions, we have had to spank one of our children for a reason that we felt warranted. Each discipline is followed by a learning discussion of what they did wrong, and what would have been the right thing to do. We allow our children to understand their choices they have made and how making better choices would have different results. I think a very important value missing in the world today is self-discipline. Discipline was a big part of my life and who I am today.

Going back to the early teen and college years of my life, I hung out with two key role models, my football buddies. They were the guys that you hang out with, that set the examples, and model your behavior. I was lucky! My best friends had respect, morals, discipline, and were straight "A" honor roll students. It was an awesome fact that they were also "smash mouth" linebackers. One was also a minister's son and was raised with a very big heart that we all loved and respected. The 3 of us knew the right way to do things with respect and discipline. We were not only successful in high school, but we carried this mind set in life, as we all created our careers and families. It is very interesting to see the attributes that made us successful back in high school, are still key values in our lives today.

Anissa and I are both from higher level educational backgrounds. We have both achieved post graduate degrees in our professions. I was raised in the public schools and Anissa attended a Catholic elementary school. We have enrolled all of our children in St. Mary Basha Catholic School. We hope to have them follow this tradition by attending Seton High School or a similar Catholic high school.

Our home is large and warm. There is plenty of room for a great game of hide and seek. It is approximately 8,000 square feet with 5-6 bedrooms and 6 bathrooms. We live on a 5 acre county island parcel. It has all kinds of kids' features like a baseball field, built in playground, pool, basketball court, and large grassy play area. It has plenty of blacktop for bike riding, roller blading and scooter riding. We open up our house to kids, our siblings, our moms and dads, cousins, etc. We have as many family gatherings as we can. We love family and bringing everyone together.

Anissa and I both have strong Catholic values and we raise our family the same. Our adopted children will be raised with the same beliefs and values as our biological children. I tried to do the "Right Things" vs "Doing Things Right." People see what your work values are because these are an extension of your home values. You want your "Leadership" to only tell you the right things to do, but set an example by your behavior. If you want to know what a person's or a business's values are, just watch their behavior. You do not have to listen to what they say, watch what they do!

"Living Leadership" is sometimes extremely difficult, but must be done on a consistent basis. Your business is a picture of your personal life. My success was initially started when I was born into my family. Then it continued with my upbringing and marriage.

When you do the right things in your business, it is because you have learned the right traits that navigate you down the correct road. Sometimes people try to minimize risk, but that is not always the right road to take, to make improvements, or accomplish items you dream about.

In our business, you have to look at consistency with your decisions with your colleagues, your peers, and your associates. You have to bring the same message to every part of your life, including your vision and values for your business. As I said previously, this is what I consider being consistent, to be doing the "Right Things vs Doing Things Right." Consistency of Life Values cross over to your Business Values. They go hand in hand.

Your values drive your family as well as your business family. If you look at the office areas here in our business, it is organized, caring, generous, and mirrors my life and culture. My success in business has been a culmination of my wife's and my life mission, to attain greater heights working together, as a family as well as the business. I run 4 businesses and still drive the kids to school and still work 8 hours a day. It is all about scheduling priorities and balance. It is important to become and stay "present" for your family.

If I look back, the road to a successful business started with an interesting 1st job. It was selling wicker and rotund baskets at a local swap meet. I knew I wanted more to life and focused on what was right and what was not right, while being exposed to the people at Amphitheater High School. During this time I was also exposed to a Health Related Organization, which introduced me to the Orthotics and Prosthetics profession, which I am in today. I brought my family values into our service business. This was a very proud moment in my life.

When I am exposed to a person's traumatic condition, I coach people through these changes in their lives. Life changing events cause significant emotional events in an individual's life. One thing that was big in my mind, was that my being the owner, I wanted to see the patient. I had a burn patient about 12 years ago. I saw surgeons and therapists to help assist this patient. I tell the patient that you may fall, but I and others will "help you up."

You have to figure out how you are going to balance your business, your family, and your personal life, to mold them into a success. Too much time spent in any one area, detracts from the success of the other areas. My wife and I have to figure out how to navigate a successful environment with soccer, football, chess, band, ballet, homework, dinners, baths, etc. for 5 kids. Like I mentioned previously, I still drive kids to school, while being responsible for 4 businesses, and a number of employees. Early in in my life, in my early 20s, I was working 18 hours per day. I was doing everything in the office and spending very little time at home. You can't continue with that process with a family and family business. It will take its toll on both.

How I maintain my success is dependent on living family values at home, as well as with any of my businesses. Maybe there is more there than just cultural background. There are family traits, religion, values and culture. When you brand a company with your vision, it is with your mission statement, and values. My 1st and 2nd companies were innovation startups. I was associated with people who had similar upbringing and backgrounds. Relationships grow with equal minded traits, values, and no fear of being mistrusted. Business staff must openly talk about how to run the business. This is in addition to how well the business is being run.

You have to create an environment for people to be successful. Be fair, open, work hard, and gain the education necded to be successful. We must get along as we must make the office a family. It is just work, as there are a lot more important things in life, other than work. The community recognizes what you do and how you do it. You do not have to tell them. (Remember my "Behavior" comment earlier?)

I hear the comment, "I love to work with Joe." You have to work to get there. You have to do the right things day in and day out to get there. It is not easy, but very rewarding. Many of my staff are young admins with whom I have built strong working relationships. We work many hours and trust each other to do the right thing for our families and the business. Building the trust for people to live in a work environment, is dependent upon having the right values, which make for a strong foundation, and a successful company.

People have values that need to be shared. In my business, we discuss monthly, quarterly and yearly goals that are supported by these values. We also do a Team Incentive Plan (TIP), where employees are not held to monthly sales goals as an "individual." When you have individual goals within a business, you pit one employee against the next. This causes behavior that is negative and hurts others. My goal in all companies, is to create opportunity for success with our business family, working as a team. I like saying, "our family of businesses."

You have to maintain flexibility in your business. Every year you have new products or services along with new people. We have to determine who is going to pay for what with their efforts. We have to determine how to control costs. I have been in business for 19 years, with the last 5 years being the most difficult. You have to determine what work ethic is required to stay in business. Others are depending on you, as well as their families.

Businesses have to "re-invent the mindset" to stay healthy and productive. You have to find the people needing you, just as you need them. I remember when I was young getting into sports. You have the right coach, the right person that leads you in the right direction, teaching you respect, sportsmanship, and a work ethic where you don't get stuff for free.

We have to keep asking the question, how can I help? When talking to kids you need to ask questions where the answers are not just yes or no. The same with your patients to help them. Ask the questions, or frame your questions, so that you really get a good feel from where they are with their affliction.

When you do the "right things, the right things" come to you. Following faith and family values, this will happen. In a small similarity, managing my home and my family, and my businesses all the same.

Giving back we see as being beneficial to our business. We apply to our church, the same aspects of our life, as we do our family and our business. We think that is a formula for making it a success. We both devote a lot of time to making our church as successful as our business.

Another area that is important to us to give back, is the area of insurance companies that can't or won't pay for our products and services. We make every effort to provide appliances to anyone that can't afford the product or service.

We work very closely with the Foundation for Burns and Trauma in Maricopa County. We are involved in the "Limbs for Lives," where we provide some type of support for the non-profit organizations. We have also found a niche for kids in the various burn camps located in Prescott, Arizona. This camp is put on by the Arizona Burn Foundation. It allows kids that have suffered traumatic burn injuries, to be able to forget about their surgeries, procedures, and hospitals, and just have some fun.

If we look back with any success that I have had in my life, it began with my parents. They built the foundation for my future successes, with my faith, family, and business. It seems that today, many people can have a business success, but not a family success. This may or may not be the result of the time devoted to their business and not their family. It is a balancing act, but when done with purpose, a very rewarding one!

**Laura Leal**
**Business Field:** Family Nurse Practitioner
**Business Name:** East Valley Family Medicine
**Current Position:** Family Nurse Practitioner

**Personal Background:**

I was born in Concord, California and then we moved to Oregon when I was 6 months old. I have an older sister, an older brother, and a younger sister. My mom is deceased, but my dad is still living in Oregon.

As far as my educational background, I graduated from Hermiston High School in 1992. Academically, I did well in school, but just did not have a lot of parental guidance. It wasn't like I was going to graduate with a "4.0" and go to Harvard or any major Ivy League school. I was on a color guard team and that was about the extent of my extra-curricular activities. I did work while in high school. My opinion is what happens from birth to high school affects decisions that you make, etc. These years are your "building blocks for success."

For some reason, I was not raised or spent any amount of time around my relatives. My dad thought that my mom's relatives were "different" and not a good influence on me. My mom always seemed to be ill. She had her first stroke at age 21. That may be one of the reasons that I chose nursing as my career. I was a caretaker for her for 10 years until her death. With the stroke, she had cancer, and was also a diabetic. But in spite of that, she gave me some "biblical" guidance and lots of love. I had divorced parents. This was about age 16 or 17. My mom moved to Arizona and my dad went to live with his then girlfriend. The girlfriend was actually our neighbor. This is when my little sister came about. This was a troubling time for me, but I did get a little sister, which was positive.

During this time, I was living with one of my particular friend's family after having a traumatic break from my family. They saw that I was in distress and offered help. While with them, they required that I attend church services. They said that you can sleep here, but you have to go to church. This is when my love of God got ignited. I paid them a little bit of rent as they could not afford to take me on. I am still friends with their daughter to this day.

While living with my friend's family, all of my belongings were in my car. My car was a 1980 Subaru station wagon. Plenty of closet space, right? But I was fortunate enough to have a part-time job at a Dairy Queen for 2 years that helped me get by financially.

People did extend warmth and love to me and I think that is why I extend that to others today. But as previously stated, I did not receive hardly any parental advice.

I was a product of the people that I was associating with. One of those associations was soon to be my husband whom I met in 1993. He was a very troubled man. I was just a young woman that had a lot of bad things happen to me, due to my inexperience of life. Being naïve and kind hearted is not always the best thing. This sometimes leads you into trouble. It was not any legal trouble for which I would go to jail, but still not good experiences from which you build a future.

Going back to when I was in high school, I never had any senior pictures, no invitations to graduation, or anything like that. I did the best I could and don't even remember how I got my cap and gown for graduation. I think that I had to borrow it from someone. The finances were very limited, so I went with what I had and let the rest go.

I did date while in high school prior to getting married, but never experienced a serious relationship with anyone. A boyfriend here and there, but nothing serious. I had a prom date and did as much as I could socially being on my own. I got married young at 19, to someone that was incredibly abusive, and I almost died from this marriage. This began one of the most difficult times in my life. I ran for years from him. The problem was that I had no point of reference of a good relationship, because I had never been out with anyone before him.

Going back to my first marriage, just about 3 months after being married, I had a miscarriage. It was not a viable pregnancy and was not greater than 24 weeks. I think this had a profoundly negative effect on my ex-husband, like it was my fault. It was as if he blamed me for losing her. What made it worse was that when I went to the doctor they told me I needed to have the baby removed. Instead of doing it that day, they sent me home and told me to come back in 3 days. I went home knowing that inside of me was a human being that would never see a real life. Looking back, I see it as a 19 year old who needed medical help and no one to advocate for her. If it happened today, I would have demanded to get in that day to have the procedure, instead of waiting 3 days. Even though I never saw her, I still feel that she is a real part of my life, and I will see her someday.

I had my first child at 20. Then I got divorced at 21. It took me about 18 months to get out of the abusive relationship, whereas other women in such relationships, often take years to get out of their situation. My daughter was 8 months old when I left. After I left my ex-husband, he became homeless in my neighborhood and started stalking me. I was on the run with my daughter for about 2 years. It is really very difficult to talk about. My daughter was the pivotal reason to get straightened out and for me to get back into school. I needed to settle things down so that I could provide for her. There were so many crazy stories in my life about this time, that I could do an entire book on these issues that plagued me. I probably should have been dead, but it appears that God had a different plan for me.

My daughter's biological father does not know her, nor did he have very much contact with her. She does not know him. This has been a positive thing for me as he was unfit for a relationship with her. My current husband has been nurturing and kind to her. Since she was 2 ½ or 3 when she met my current husband, she never really remembers a life without him. To her he is her real father.

When I look at this, and talk about this, I want people who read this, to know that I did not think that I was equipped to make the life and marriage decisions in front of me. There were no drugs, drinking, or partying. I was just true to my faith. When I met this man in church, my ex-husband and father of my daughter, I did not realize his level of mental illness. Turns out he was not the right one at all. But I did not realize that at the time.

I was naive about my first husband, as he was living in a halfway house when we met. This halfway house was part of the church that I had been attending. I had no idea what a halfway house was or the purpose or concept of one. I think that this was a fatal flaw in the church organization. I was born into the Catholic faith but only attended church on Christmas and Easter. Also, I think that the lack of guidance from my parents did impact my decision-making later on in life, with my choice of my first husband being an example. I love my parents and do not want to talk ill of them, but it just seems that they were not equipped, to guide me to make better decisions in life. Coming from a divorced family, entering into a bad marriage, divorced, followed for a period of time, harassed, and choked, takes its toll on a person.

Before going into the nursing profession, I felt as though I had fought a war. But in having the relationship that I had in my life with my parents and 1st husband, it prepared me for what I would be seeing in nursing. Knowing what I had been through, allowed me to understand what I needed to do to escape that life that I wanted to leave behind. The answer was education, which propelled me towards any success that I have had in my life.

I am not afraid of saying anything that I have said, because I think that it helps myself and other young women to avoid some of the same situations that I had been exposed to in my life. God and education are a pretty remarkable process to help bring a person that lived the life that I did, back to some sort of reasonableness, so to speak. My 1-2 punch is faith and education. There is a lot of strength in people who have been "damaged." A few tough years made for a very wonderful future.

My daughter lives at home and is a top salesperson for Victoria Secret. I have a stepdaughter that I raised for 17 years. She was 8 years old when I got her. I now have a wonderful blended family.

I started at a community college in 1998. I obtained my LPN degree in 2002 and my RN degree in 2003. I went back for my Bachelor's degree from 2005-2007 and earned it from Grand Canyon University.

I went right into my Master's program in 2007 at Grand Canyon University and graduated with my NP degree in 2010. Right after that, I started my Doctoral studies in 2014 at Arizona State University. I will be receiving a Doctorate of Nursing Practice degree in the fall of 2016 or spring of 2017 depending on timing of courses etc.

It has been a very long, albeit rewarding process. I have been going to school for over a decade! I started working in a hospital setting about 14 years ago as a Health Unit Secretary in a high risk labor and delivery unit on the night shift.

Then I worked as a Certified Nursing Assistant (CNA). From there I took a position as a patient care technician. Then I worked as an LPN through the last year of nursing school. I worked 7-8 years in the ICU from a new grad RN position to the ICU Manager. During my job as lead ICU nurse I worked my way through graduate school. I can honestly say I have done every type of clinical work from a secretary to a health care PCP. During all of this I began teaching and mentoring other nurses through becoming a hospital clinical instructor.

A local physician named Dr. Gill Holland was looking for a Nurse Practitioner (NP) at Grand Canyon University. He stated that he wanted a "good student." That was me! I came to meet Dr. Holland in January when I was finishing up my clinical rotation for my FNP degree. He hired me right out of school.

What led to my success was my vision to demonstrate keen insight and exquisite foresight in the field of nursing. In this arena, you help people understand that they can prolong their life or prolong their death. You can help them make that decision. I think that my background made me strong enough to help others in these decisions.

I will prepare myself beyond what was previously possible for nurses, becoming a leader in my field. I plan to advance the profession of nursing through education and innovation. I will lead, mentor, and precept new nurses through servant leadership. I intend to place myself in the path of perpetual knowledge, providing the best possible care available. As an RN my responsibilities were:

- Navigating electronic medical records
- Physician collaboration
- Telephone triage
- Daily patient scheduling including labs
- Imaging
- Surgical and bedside procedures
- Becoming proficient in all documentation, record maintenance, and patient confidentiality

- Attaining expert levels for critical skill set including rapid response team, code team, difficult IV insertion resource, ICU preceptor for new RN's, and relief charge nurse

In 2008 I was awarded Nursing Leader of the Year, while working at Banner Mesa, now called Banner Gateway Hospital. The reason I received the award was:

- My ability to administer the ICU at Banner Mesa
- Writing protocols and improved various systems
- The ability and initiative to teach/train new nurses
- Kindness extended to the nurses and related well to them

If you look at what I have done as a Family Nurse Practitioner, it includes:

- Taking health histories and providing complete physical examinations
- Diagnosing and treating many common acute and chronic problems
- Interpreting lab results and X-rays
- Prescribing and manage medications
- Providing health teaching and counseling to support healthy lifestyle behaviors
- Referring patients to other health professionals as required
- Establishing in-patient assessments, counseling, and medication education

- Documenting care plans for diagnosis and administration of treatment procedures

Regarding my medical background, I have a well-rounded work history:

- Family Nurse Practitioner at Ocotillo Family Medicine
- Associate Faculty at the University of Phoenix
- Critical Care Registered Nurse (Clinical Manager) at Banner Gateway Medical Center
- Banner Fellow's Nursing Instructor at Banner Health
- Adjunct Faculty for Maricopa Community Colleges/Nursing Instructor

Let's face it, becoming an RN with a BS degree shows some success. But to build on that success requires you to become pro-active in additional areas. Becoming an FNP was an extension of my initial success as an RN. To maintain what I have already gained, I am continuing my education as previously mentioned.

Maintaining and building on my relationship with my husband and kids has helped me in my success within my professional life. My husband is a skilled welder and we have been together for 15 years. His specialty is fabrication and he is very talented in this area. My husband and I decided together right after we were married, that only one of us could afford to go to school. Since he did not have the desire to further his formal education, because of the skilled trade that he was in, we decided that I would further my education.

Since I now make more money than him, we all know that this sometimes causes "issues" to creep up in a relationship. It did not in ours. By having me further my education, he feels supported, loved, and that the family as a whole is benefiting from my education being extended. My husband has communicated to me that his support has provided me the opportunity to go forward with my formal education. There has never been an issue in this area. He did not want the glory for himself, as he was perfectly fine with my educational advancement. He always encouraged me and never felt as though he was left out.

I am working towards becoming an author in a Clinical Publishing Research arena. I think that I am still looking for that "Dream Job" which may turn out to be running an NP Clinic. I think that my Nursing Program was very fragmented. The reason for this is because I first got my 2 year degree, then my bachelors, then on to my Master's degree. Sometimes you have to fragment your school to give time to your kids, to assist them, and also you husband, as in my case. It is a balancing act to make it all come together and be successful.

Based on my success I have been able to give back to others. I have mentored several students personally. I continue to mentor NP students through various universities. I also taught at University of Phoenix as adjunct faculty. I received a leader of the year award from the ICU in 2008, I was on several committees in my hospital days helping to write protocols and establish rapid response teams. I am also interested in teaching at the community college level. I also give objects and items to charitable organizations.

I am doing some charity work in downtown Phoenix and also solicited for HopeFest 2015. What this organization does is to provide thousands of people with *free* medical, dental, vision, food, housing, haircuts, clothing, personal care products, employment services, tax preparation, fitness training, and child safety needs. Finally, I pray for the sick and ask for spiritual guidance frequently. As I have said previously, this helped me through my life and I consider this as giving back to others.

**Michael Palumbo**
**Business Field:** Litigation Attorney
**Business Name:** Jennings, Strouss, & Salmon, PLC
Special Counsel
**Current Position:** Retired

**Personal Background:**

I went to a small, co-ed Catholic high school in Belmar, New Jersey, named St. Rose High School. I graduated in 1964 in a class of around 150. The school had a college prep focus. We were taught mostly by nuns. Discipline and academics were the orders of the day. Sports were also very important. I got my initial involvement with soccer during high school.

My parents taught me all the positive values that helped me through life. They were very moral people, and they passed those morals on to their children. My dad was a selfless person, who was dedicated to his family. He sacrificed his personal interest by taking over his father's florist business after my grandfather's death and running that business for his mother. He worked 6 ½ days a week, and rarely took time off for vacations. He did his best to provide material goods and opportunities for my mom, my brother and me. My mom provided order and stability in our lives, and most significantly, she provided a sense of family with her extended family. She had 8 siblings, and I had close to 30 cousins. These aunts, uncles and cousins were (and are) significant parts of my life. Having such a close extended family is (and was) a blessing.

I went to La Salle College (now University) in Philadelphia, an all-male Christian Brothers institution. I studied political science-education. I was a fairly good student with a B+ average. I played varsity soccer in college and was co-captain of a not-so-good team.

After graduating from La Salle, I spent some time substitute teaching in the schools around my home, including my alma mater, St. Rose. When the American History teacher at St. Rose left school at mid-year, I was asked to take over his classes for the remainder of the year, which I did. He was also the varsity soccer coach, so, given my background in soccer, I was offered the opportunity to coach the varsity team the next season.

I mostly taught Twentieth Century American History. I also taught World History for one year, but did not really like it, so I gave that up, and started teaching elective courses. I taught two electives, one each semester – American Government and International Relations (Peace Studies). This was during the latter part of the Vietnam War, when students were somewhat politicized. The classes were exciting.

Despite disadvantages in terms of facilities and the number of students, we had a very successful soccer program. We played a challenging schedule against bigger schools, but we always ranked high in our county rankings and often in the state rankings. We won 3 state championships in the eight years I was the coach. There were many lessons, but two that stand out were: (1) hard work and preparation overcome disadvantages and (2) selfless dedication to the common good contributes to achievement. Although I liked the students and loved coaching soccer, I left teaching because of typical frustrations:

the pay was poor, and there was little positive reinforcement. If I could have continued coaching soccer without teaching, I would have.

After teaching, I went directly to Notre Dame Law School, where I graduated "Cum Laude" in 1981. Upon law school graduation, I took a job at the largest and one of the oldest law firms in Phoenix, Arizona. I stayed there for 4 years. I learned many aspects of how to be a good lawyer; however, the practice at that firm was all consuming. There was no balance, and time for personal interests and family was much too limited. Therefore, I sought a position at a firm where work-life balance was more available. I found that at my present firm, where I have been practicing for almost 30 years.

I have tried to live my life according to 3 guiding principles:

### Humility with Excellence

By this I mean try to be your best in everything you do, but do not let success get in the way of ability to relate to others. An example of this principle applied to my professional career is that although I have been named to numerous "Best Lawyer" lists, I have never let that influence how I interacted with peers, clients, or adversaries. I always try to treat others as though they were my equals.

### Servant Leadership

This principle suggests that the focus of efforts is not personal gain, but the betterment of your society. I have been involved in leadership positions in many organizations, including my law firm and charitable organizations. I have approached those positions with the idea that you never use the positions that you hold to foster your own benefit; always look to better the group.

## Live Life with Passion and Compassion

This refers to approaching responsibilities with determination tempered with concern for others. If you approach things with passion alone, you can get carried away, sometimes to the unnecessary detriment of others; but, if you moderate your passion with compassion, you will not hurt people in the process of pursuing your job/hobby/interest.

Do not get ahead of yourself; do not lose focus on the fact that any success you have gained is the result of many circumstances, often including luck and the efforts of others.

Really, success comes from always trying to act according to the guiding principles. But, two things that lawyers must do to maintain continued good relationships with clients are to communicate regularly and promptly and never hide bad news.

Giving back involves the concept of "Servant Leadership."

I have tried to give back by contributing "pro bono" legal services to the poor and to friends who need help. I have coordinated my law firm's legal clinic at one of the local human services organizations; I have taken pro bono cases for the county Volunteer Lawyers Program and I have volunteered on many State Bar Association committees.

I also try to be a "mentor" to young lawyers and teach professionalism and responsibility to the community. The approach I take varies and includes one on one advising, group counseling for my firm, for the State Bar Association and for individual lawyers, often alums from Notre Dame Law School.

I also support many groups with time and effort, depending on their focus and needs. Some of the things I have been involved in are Rotary, Special Olympics, local youth athletic clubs, Arizona State Bar Association, national breast cancer fund raisers, and Maggie's Place (support for unwed mothers).

**Natalie Sayer**
**Business Field:** Leadership Consulting
**Business Name:** The Blair David Company
**Current Position:** Founder/Principal

**Personal Background:**

I was raised in a small town outside of Dayton, Ohio. Many of the lessons I learned in both my family and town have carried me forward in my life as a leader. These lessons are the foundation to the success I have been fortunate enough to have:

- Every person has unique value.
- Treat others as you would want to be treated.
- Try new things.
- Travel to learn and grow.
- Learn your whole life.
- Adjust yourself accordingly.
- There is honor in a strong work ethic.
- Creativity is important.
- Laugh often.
- Be thankful for what you have.
- Give back - Share your gifts and talents.
- Appreciate the people in your life.
- Pay attention - how you show up impacts others for good or not.

**Beginnings and Background**

My extended family was from humble beginnings. My dad was the first in his family to get a college degree. He spent most of his career at General Motors. This enabled us to travel on family vacations; our goal was to take pictures of all 50 state capitols. (At this writing, we have six left.) When I was in junior high school, my dad had assignments that took him around the world. In my mind, I wanted to be able to travel the world like that when I "grew up." For both of my parents, it was important to create a strong foundation for my older brother and me. My mom went to St. Joseph's Commercial High School. When she graduated, she worked as a commercial food broker and taught dancing.

She was the engine in our family. She supported my dad as he was in college completing his masters. She worked until she was 8 ½ months pregnant with my brother. While she stayed home when we were young, she eased back into work by teaching dancing again. When I was in fifth grade, she took some college courses, to refresh her skills, before she went back into the work world. Her goal and dream was that both my brother and I would have college educations. So, she worked to fund that dream.

While both my parents actively supported us in our schooling and activities, my mom was the one, who instilled the value of an education in me. She received that value from her father, David. He grew up in an orphanage until age 13, when the boys left. He completed two years of pre-seminary training, which was the equivalent of high school at that time. Although not quite of age, he managed to enter the US Army Calvary for WWI; they signed the Armistice on his 18th birthday. Later he would work as a polisher at National Cash Register. Through the Depression, he did what he needed to do to support his family, including driving a pie truck.

Although he had limited formal education, he was a lifelong learner. As a young man, he learned all the trades required to build a house for his in-laws. He learned how to customize cars. In his later years, he learned how to water ski and bowl. After his first stroke he learned how to ride a three-wheel bicycle, when the two-wheeler would no longer suffice. Even after more severe strokes partially paralyzed him, he was still learning - to write, speak, and draw again.

I can remember speaking on the phone with him after he had moved to Florida; in his clear Irish tenor, he would always ask, "How are you doing in school?" One of my last memories of my Gramps was on his last birthday. He was not having a good day at all. We were to go to my senior year marching band concert. I had arranged to have the band director surprise him with a birthday song. In spite of not feeling well, when the song played, he put on a smile, tried to doff his hat with his paralyzed hand, and express gratitude for the song and appreciation to the crowd. Within a month, he was gone. While I learned many lessons from my Gramps, the most important were tenacity, applied learning, humor, and a generosity of spirit.

While public figures can be inspiring, in my life my greatest inspiration and role models for leadership and life success came from everyday people, like my parents and Gramps.

At the time, Bellbrook, my town, was a one traffic light town, where we all knew each other. I started kindergarten and graduated high school with about 75% of the same people. Although no place is ideal, growing up where and when I did afforded me many opportunities to develop leadership skills and a pattern of achievement at an early age. Whether it was tutoring fellow classmates to master their multiplication tables, gaining parts in musicals, or "adjusting myself accordingly" when life did not happen as I wished, I took every opportunity I could to practice and grow as a leader in life.

My favorite place in town was Winters Library. There wasn't a lot to do in Bellbrook. The nearest mall was 20 minutes away. We had no fast food places where we could "hang out." Walking to the pharmacy for candy, riding your bike in the summer to the swim club and playing with friends on the street were some of my favorite activities. But the best thing in my world was to go to the library. The library was a place that opened up the world beyond my small town and fostered imagination and creativity.

When I was ten, I went to the head librarian, Mrs. Blair, and asked, "How old do you have to be to work here?"

"Thirteen."

"I will see you on my thirteenth birthday!"

Sure enough, on my thirteenth birthday, I filled out the application and secured the next available four-year position as a page at the library. I loved working with Mrs. Blair, because she didn't see me as a thirteen-year-old kid. She believed in me and taught me to do things beyond my job description. What a great role model to have as a first boss!

No matter how busy she was, Mrs. Blair took the time to listen to people, young and old. She was quick with a laugh or a smile. She epitomized customer service excellence. She undertook causes she cared about, like the preservation of historical documents housed at the library. But one of the most amazing things to me is the strength, courage, and tenacity she demonstrated, as she fought cancer at the same time. While we worked together, she did not allow that fight to get in the way of how she showed up as a leader. I still admire her tenacity and grace.

One other advantage in Bellbrook was the school system. We had great teachers and the class sizes were small enough that you could learn and try new activities. I will say that for me it was an early "life-lab" where it was safe to risk and step out of your comfort zone. One of these growth experiences was our class trip to New York City during junior and senior years, with the English and Drama teacher Miss Long. These trips created in me a passion for big cities, the arts, and Broadway. I believe successful people are well rounded and willing to stretch beyond comfort to grow.

During our senior year, we could take a day to explore potential career paths. My guidance counselors, Mr. Wenclewicz and Ms. Martin, arranged for me to spend that day at the Inland Division of General Motors. By the end of that day, and with the encouragement of Mr. Risner my Chemistry teacher, I pursued a cooperative education job and the study of engineering at the University of Dayton. That year I was one of two people from my school who received co-op jobs with General Motors. Two weeks after graduation, I was working on a rubber press making bad parts.

No matter how hard I tried, they just wouldn't come out of the machine correctly. After being screamed at for my work, I learned an important lesson "don't blame the operator first." Turns out that the machine wasn't properly aligned, so even the most experienced operator could not make quality parts.

One of the best aspects of my co-op experience was before I had my university degree; I had broad exposure to almost all of the functional areas of the division. Even though I studied engineering, I rotated through human resources, purchasing/supply chain, quality, manufacturing, engineering, sales, and finance. I also had my first international assignment in Mexico. These experiences were an amazing foundation to launch my career.

## Education and Career

I have two engineering degrees: Bachelors of Mechanical Engineering from the University of Dayton and Masters of Science Manufacturing Systems Engineering from the University of Michigan Rackham School. Beyond formal degrees, I have taken a plethora of work related training, which gave me skills to facilitate strategy, organizational development, and team building sessions. When I decided to start my own endeavor, I completed Coachu and Corporate Coachu (Coachu is an International Coach Federation approved coaching school).

I have found that curiosity is a great trait to have as a lifelong learner. I read voraciously, take classes in subjects that interest me, and can expand my perspective. The internet has opened so many options as well, from YouTube videos or TED talks to MOOCs. Yet one of my favorite ways to learn is through travel.

You can not only learn about people and cultures, but learn a lot about yourself in the process. Some of my greatest experiences were in countries where we did not speak the same language. Let's face it, it goes for English in other parts of the world too. As Oscar Wilde wrote in *The Canterville Ghost* (1887), "We have really everything in common with America nowadays except, of course, language."

I spent 15 ½ years with General Motors working in the USA and Mexico. During that time, General Motors went through many reorganizations and consolidations of divisions. I was fortunate to be at the right place at the right time and worked on many interesting assignments, with progressively more responsibility. Some of these assignments included:

- a co-op assignment in Mexico (I spoke no Spanish and had not lived away from Ohio)
- internal consultant in a department that would today be considered a forerunner to Lean and Six Sigma,
- design release engineer on GMs early electric vehicle (which is now in the Smithsonian),
- plant start-up lead again in Mexico
- Industrial Engineering manager on a plant conversion team that won the GM President's Award
- My last assignment, the staff member tasked with coordinating the sale of the Mexican Seating Operations.

After the sale, I worked at Lear Corporation as an Engineering Manager, Program Manager, Six

Sigma Black Belt, and internal consultant. In 2002, I reached a point in life where this path no longer fit my future goals and dreams. I started to plan my next steps and in 2003, I opened I-Emerge Coaching, Inc. a leadership coaching and consulting practice in Surprise, Arizona. Recognizing when something has run its course and having faith it is time to change, has contributed to my success. Sure change can be scary, but it is the only way to grow and stay relevant.

Opening your own business is an education unto itself. I have learned many lessons and realized the importance of the core values I learned growing-up. I have run my own venture for over 13 years. My childhood dream to travel the world has become a reality; I have been fortunate enough to work in 16 countries, in English and Spanish. I have trained thousands of people in concepts ranging from leadership to Lean.

I am the lead author of two editions of <u>Lean For Dummies</u> (Wiley 2007 and 2012). I have also helped leaders to develop strategy and improve their leadership capabilities. I have taught in the Master's program for Webster University. I have been in a movie and have spoken to groups as large as 2800. I have acted as a lead performer in over 10 plays and moderated statewide political debates. As I have progressed in my career, I have realized the importance of being a well-rounded individual, taking risks and bringing all my talents to work.

While it would be easy to list all positive outcomes, I believe that success also lies in the significant learning moments. Learning how to be an entrepreneur, after spending my entire adult life in large companies, did not come without significant lessons: How do you do sales and marketing? Who are your clients? Where do you find them? What are you willing to try to keep cash flowing? Who is in your network that can help you? What do you do when a supplier suddenly goes out of business with your money? How do you stay in touch with people? How do you stay relevant? How do you relate to different cultures and generations?

I have made mistakes, learned, made more mistakes, and learned some more in the years I have been in business. I know I will learn even more in the future. So what does this have to do with success, when it sounds like a failure? Resilience and tenacity. I have found it isn't how hard I fall that is important. It is how fast I can fail, learn, and try a different course or as my Gramps would say, "Adjust yourself accordingly and roll with the punches."

In Lean terms, it is a Plan-Do-Check-Act/Adjust cycle. My husband and I joke that life is an engineering problem. We just have to know what problem we are trying to solve, find the right solution for the situation, then go. I also believe that successful people stay curious, are lifelong learners, and have a vision backed up with actions.

In 2012, a trusted advisor and long-time client suggested it was time to reinvent the business. Based on that conversation I made several changes, including renaming the business to The Blair David Company; the name honors two of my early leadership role models – Mrs. Blair and Gramps Cleary. The focus of the business now is Pointillism Leadership™ our model to develop leaders for every moment and improve leadership outcomes.

Who knows what will be next?  One thing that I have learned in my career is to be open to new opportunities, do your best with them, and be flexible to change course or learn something new. I've also realized there is a balancing act between patience and action. When the timing is right, things seem to flow; when it isn't patience is required or you end up burning through resources trying to force outcomes.

The further I progress in my career, I realize that success is a multifaceted concept. For me it is both an external and internal concept. Externally it happens with the people we develop and influence, the opportunities wc take advantage of, and the accomplishment we achieve along the way. Internally, who we are and who we believe we can become fuels our success.

I have had the good fortune of working for Fortune 150 companies; GM was ranked in the top five when I worked there. I was part of history while working on the first production Electric Vehicle program, now in the Smithsonian. I was part of a major transformation with the team who won the GM President's Award. I learned about the "ups and downs" of mergers and acquisitions when I led the plant sales team.  I wrote a popular business book. Mostly, all of these accomplishments have taught me to take risks, seize opportunities at the moment, use all of your experiences, and the importance of people and leadership. For behind all successes are people and everyday leaders.

While external success can be measured in financial terms, organizational status, or accomplishments, for me an even more important measure of success is leadership impact. All of us lead in every moment of every day - or not. You may or may not ever know your real impact, but sometimes something happens to show you a glimpse. My glimpse came in the form of a Facebook friend request a few years ago. "Mario S would like to be your friend." At first, I did not recognize the name. I went through my mental contacts file; the only Mario S I could think of was the supervisor of lift truck repair from my college co-op assignment in Mexico. I accepted the request and asked, "Mario from Matamoros?"

"Yes, sunshine! I wanted to thank you."

I was perplexed. For I had no idea why he would be thanking me. If anything, I should be thanking him, for he helped in so many ways, not just language and culture. (I had no Spanish abilities at the time.) He went on to tell me that through our conversations, I helped him with his English, to understand how to work with Americans better, and how to think about work differently. Because of those four months we spent in lift truck repair, he was able to be more successful for many years to come. I was humbled and grateful for this exchange. While I was "just being me" in those conversations, I realize that how you show up in the small moments, when no one is watching, shows your character. Your character is part of your success.

Since the beginning of my career, a global perspective and an interest in all forms of culture have been important to me. To be successful in today's connected world, you have to have an awareness about customers and colleagues, what are their protocols and norms, your biases, and how to navigate both the similarities and differences. I had a session with 22 people, 8 nationalities represented, predominately engineers, who worked for a large multinational company.

The second day we had a mutiny because most of the participants were thinking, this is too "American" and it won't work here. This session was a positive psychology based leadership workshop. There was nothing wrong with the tools, but they were so culturally different - company culture, professional culture, and, of course, national culture. We navigated through it, but if I wasn't respectful, curious, empathetic, aware, patient and grounded, it could have had a very different outcome.

### Giving back
*"Those whom we support hold us up in life."* (Marie Von Ebner-Eschenbach)

As I reflect on my career and life so far, I am where I am and have had the successes I have had because others have supported me. My family instilled in me a spirit of giving back. As a professional, I continue to give back. Like many, I give money to charity and causes I believe in, like the arts and literacy. In addition, I give my time. To "Reading for the Blind" in Michigan and Arizona, I gave my voice.

I have been an active member in several professional organizations, like the National Speakers Association where I've been a chapter board member and treasurer. I have been active as a member and leader with the Arizona Women's Partnership, a small non-profit serving at risk women and children in Arizona. I will continue to look for opportunities to share my gifts and talents with the world.

Developing people is another way to give back. I have done this in many different ways, but it all boils down to coaching and mentoring. While leading a team in Mexico, I was trying to learn Spanish, while my team was trying to learn English. We created a weekly "English day" to augment their classes. One day each week, we would practice English. The "fine" for not speaking English on English day was you had to fill the candy jar. I think I ended up with the most fines on English day!

Within a year, we had all improved our language skills and had become closer as a team. My team mentored me as well, helping me to understand the language and culture of Mexico. This makes me think about another success factor; successful people are not afraid to receive constructive feedback. It helps you grow and see blind spots, if you are willing to open your eyes.

In Arizona, I hired a friend from the theater world to help me with administrative work in my business. As time passed, I was not seeing the progress on the project, and he started to have attendance and punctuality issues. I discovered that this was not the first job where he had this issue. I had to address the situation in a constructive manner. For me this is another success factor, deal with issues constructively before they fester.

We went for coffee. When we left the office, I wasn't even sure he wanted to continue working with me. Once we reaffirmed that he did and reviewed the expectations, I went into a mentor - coach mode.

I said to him, "Based on what you have told me, this is not your 1st job where you have had an attendance issue." He agreed. Next I asked, "Do you want to change this behavior pattern?" He said he did. "Then what is getting in your way of being successful?" He then revealed issues outside of work that he was dealing with. "It may not be an option on every job that you have, but it is an option here to change your work hours."

Once we established his new working hours, I asked him if he would call if he were going to be late. He said that he could do that. That was an initial step for mc to mentor him in a behavioral change. So we ended up working through this issue, not making it about the person, but making it about the behavior.

I believe that most people are not inherently bad, but their behavior patterns can be bad. At the end of our conversation he thanked me. He said that in all of the jobs that he had ever had, he had never had a supervisor take the time to believe in him and be developmental in any way. He later went on to work for a Vegas headliner, where his new behavior pattern made him successful.

Another experience, where I think I learned as much as my mentee did, happened in Detroit. I tutored a freshman in high school who had 4th grade skills in math and reading. We started out with a basic discussion, "What are your dreams?" Having a dream or a goal I think enables success. You may not have the answer about how to achieve it, but it sets the direction in which you can focus your energy and activities. She said she wanted to be a stockbroker because they made a lot of money. Not wanting to crush her dream based on her current skill set, I brought her information about "a day in the life of a stockbroker." Once she read it, she decided it sounded boring, so we looked for a new dream.

About 2 months into our sessions, she showed me a letter that she had written to her cousin. The tutoring program was strictly about academic performance, so I asked what she wanted me to do with it. Check spelling and grammar or what? This letter contained sex, drugs, gangs, fights, and other things that were so foreign from my life experience and I wouldn't wish on anyone, especially a kid. What I did next was go to the administrator of the girl's program and ask her to talk to my student's mom, her only parent, and see if I could take her daughter on educational mentor outings. This girl needed more than what she was getting in her life at that time. I thought that one-on-one time with a professional person could show her what could be possible in life with an education. As a leader, you have to be willing to step up and act, where others won't.

Once her mom agreed to the idea, the first thing that we did was go see *Crouching Tiger* and *Hidden Dragon*. As soon as we got in the car, it was as if a light bulb came on inside of her. This normally stoic and sullen girl came alive. I chose the movie because she was interested in Asian culture, and she would have to read subtitles. Then we went to an upscale Chinese restaurant, where she could have a good meal and practice table etiquette.

About this time the Harry Potter movies were just starting to come out, so I got her to start reading the books. Our deal was if she read the first books over the summer, we would go to see the movie in the fall. But before we went to the movie, I was going to quiz her on the books. She loved the books and could answer all of the questions! She told me she got grief from her school friends for lugging huge books around in her backpack, but she didn't care because the books were so good she couldn't stop reading.

Throughout the two years we worked together we went to museums, movies, and arts events. We set some life and academic goals. She moved her skills by 4 grades. I am still very proud of her. While I guided from the side, she planned her future. When I moved, she was enrolled in school to become a pastry chef. While I have lost track of where she is, I would like to think she was better prepared for life, because of the time we spent together.

My most recent mentoring venture is through my alma mater, the University of Dayton. I am mentoring a female engineering student. Once again, I am learning as much as the person I am mentoring.

I believe that success does not happen alone. I have been blessed with people, who have believed in me. I have been blessed with growth and development opportunities. I have been blessed with a strong sense of work ethic, values and leadership. All of these started with my family and the people in my town and continued with various people and mentors throughout my life.

I don't think life or career success can be wrapped up into a neat formula, because life is messy and unpredictable. What may help to navigate though is to leverage your strengths and skills. Learn every day. Stay curious. "Adjust yourself accordingly" in the face of adversity. Stretch beyond your comfort zone. Courageously face your fears. Dream of new possibilities, take risks, make plans and set them in action. Laugh often. Show gratitude, give back, see the value in others, and lead with integrity even when no one is watching. As a successful leader in life, "How will you lead in every moment?"

**Pat Stoltze**
**Business Field:** United States Army Officer (Retired) / Insurance Agent / Purchaser / Senior Army Instructor - High School Educator (Retired)
**Business Name**: The United States Army. Country Companies Insurance Company. McDonald Douglas Aircraft Company. Trevor G. Browne High School. Marcos de Niza High School.
**Current Position**: Retired

**Personal Background:**

I grew up in Wood River, Illinois. It is a small refinery town of about 11,000 people along the Mississippi River due north of St. Louis, Missouri. My father was an architect; my mother was a stay-at-home mom.

I went to a public kindergarten and attended elementary school at St. Bernard's Catholic School in Wood River, Illinois. I graduated from Marquette Catholic High School in Alton, Illinois in 1967. I was taught by Ursuline sisters at both. One of the things I remember especially about St. Bernard's was that we had to attend Mass daily. There was a man who sat in the far right front pew who also attended daily. Forty years later he told me that during World War II in the Pacific, he went ashore with the US Marines at Tarawa, Saipan, and Okinawa. Joe was simply fulfilling a promise to God!

I have always heard that a person truly only has a very few close friends. My buds growing up attended the same schools that I did. I kept contact with only a very few of them. One just passed away. He was a US Army Viet Nam Veteran and the mayor of Wood River. The second was also an Army Viet

Nam Veteran and an employee of Standard Oil Company. A third was an Air Force Veteran of Viet Nam who worked as an independent pipe fitter. These last two gents currently live in the upper Midwest. Twenty years ago, my wife Joanne and I met another couple at our church's fundraising meeting and have been friends ever since. We recently toured France, Germany and, Austria together.

We were a middle class family with staunch Catholic and Mid-America values. My father taught me his work ethic. He set the standard of how hard one had to work to become a success. My mother was wonderful though she was no-nonsense. I knew that they both loved me. We rarely displayed affection back then like we do today. My parents were married for 51 years. They set the example for what it meant to be devoted to each other.

I have three other brothers and one sister. My twin brother and I are the only siblings living in Arizona; the others are still in the St. Louis area. They have all achieved successful lives in the business sector. My twin and I are the oldest; my sister is the youngest. She was born when I was twenty! Not surprisingly, I am closest to my twin. We get together for lunch frequently. Now that we are both recently retired, I suspect we will conduct occasional road trips to explore those parts of the southwest that we have missed so far.

Growing up, I preferred to be outside hiking in the woods, riding bikes on 40-mile trips, playing sandlot baseball or football than remaining indoors. Baseball would become my lifelong pursuit between my 8th and 19th years. No one trained harder than I did. I maintained contact with my baseball coach through the years. He taught me that dedication and hard work were necessary traits to be a winner. He dedicated at least three mornings per week coaching our practices after finishing the graveyard shift at Standard Oil. He coached us for six straight years. The lessons he taught us exceeded the fundamentals of baseball; he also taught us teamwork, dedication, and sportsmanship. These lessons I would employ throughout my life. We just lost Coach Don Wolf in 2014.

I grew up a St. Louis Cardinal Baseball fan. I can still name the starting line up every year during the 60's. It was a real thrill to go to a game and see Stan Musial hit a home run over the right field pavilion roof. I can still see Roberto Clemente hitting a line drive off Bob Gibson's ankle, breaking it. In 2015 I mentioned this to Hall of Famer, Bob Gibson, at a photo session at the National Children's Cancer Society Annual Evening with the Cardinals. He said that he sure remembered it too! My wife and I attend this event annually to support my brother who is CEO of the organization.

Our community boasted a most unique feature: a block-long swimming pool provided by Standard Oil Company. I learned to swim there. This was also the hang out for all the kids every day during my elementary and junior high years.

During my high school years, I was fairly shy around the girls, but I did have a girlfriend from time-to-time. I was very respectful to them. As a matter of fact, three years ago at my 45th high school reunion, a female classmate came up to me and told me that she thought I was pretty stuck up in school. I told her she mistook that for my lack of confidence. I was actually quite taken with the lady as a teenager (sister-in-law to a former US Attorney General), but I couldn't express it.

I was not particularly studious. I did improve as I matured. I was terrified of speaking in public. Fortunately, as I got older, I appreciated the relevancy of school, which materially improved my grades. And, thanks to the Army, I worked out my public speaking phobia.

I remember liking to play Army as a kid. I never imagined that I would spend 23 years serving our country. I was probably pretty self-centered, but not as team-oriented as I would become after joining the Army. I stayed out of trouble because I feared my parents and had respect for the law and God.

My parents and grandparents were conservative Republicans. My grandmother was quite bigoted, though I do not remember my grandfather ever saying anything negative about any person; my parents were very tolerant and taught us likewise. Beliefs were changing. I think it helped that my high school was fairly diverse.

Since my junior high days, I liked hanging out at the local airport. I could watch the planes take off and land all day long. I knew that I would fly someday.

The Viet Nam War permeated and overshadowed everything about my junior high and high school years. My high school years were 1963-1967, the build-up years of the War. My university days were 1967-1971, the heavy fighting years. It is true that I stayed in school and tried my very best to prepare myself for adult life and possible armed

111

service following graduation. The talk was: once we graduate, we will be headed for Viet Nam! This made it extremely hard to concentrate on studies and especially to take any relationships seriously. But, since I was in ROTC, I knew I would eventually be entering military service.

Any success that I achieved through my life began with working for my dad. I better work or I don't get paid! My mother said if I don't work, I won't eat! I believed both of them! We lived on the bluff overlooking the Mississippi River Valley. The property was studded with oak tree stumps. They needed removal. So my dad gave me a hand ax and a shovel and told me to take them out. Having incurred a number of shoulder injuries playing football, this was his idea of therapy for me. As difficult and tedious as this was, it had its healing effect.

On many weekends I worked for my grandfather who also had a property on the bluff overlooking the Mississippi River. He taught me mission-orientation. Here is the job. Figure it out. Get it done. Most of the work was gardening, brush clearing, and spreading manure. The volume of work, working conditions, and his expectations made those Saturdays fairly stressful.

I also learned to look before I leap. One day I was tasked with conducting a control burn on the bluff. As I was managing some fire close to the cliff, I came into contact with some very loose debris that slid down the bluff with me on it. It and I went over the side! I fell 40 feet to sloping ground below. Had it been to the left or right, I could have fallen 100-200 feet. That was a close call. The Good Lord protected me that day!

During college, I worked for Bell Telephone Company. I learned the necessity to arrive on time. I would be given a set of orders to pick up telephones no longer in service. Once I went to this house that I thought was no longer occupied. No one answered the door, so I forced my entrance through a back screen door. I went into the kitchen and removed the phone.

I continued on to other home sites to do the same thing. When I returned to the garage, my boss met me at my truck, and chewed me out. It seems that a lady was asleep in her bedroom at the first house with a gun under her pillow! Good thing I worked quietly. I learned not to take an order so seriously and to not break into anybody's home. The Lord protected me a second time.

I earned my BS degree in Marketing at Arizona State University in 1971. Compared to my peers, I led a very Spartan existence at ASU. Since ASU was a land grant school, all males had to take two years of ROTC. I made the decision my junior year to continue into Advanced ROTC. My senior year, I participated in the ROTC Flight Program earning my Private Pilot License, proving to the Army that I was competent to attend flight training at its convenience. I was the only student of 13 who completed this training simply because I was committed.

Upon graduating from ASU and commissioning as a second lieutenant in the US Army, I fully expected to be eventually sent to Viet Nam. I was sent to Fort Knox, Kentucky for the Armor Officer's Basic Course (tank training); then sent to Parachute and Ranger training as well. I volunteered for Ranger Training because an instructor at ASU advised me to get all the infantry training I could to prepare me for Viet Nam.

Ranger training was the most arduous 9 weeks of my life. I must admit that God intervened a third time on my behalf, when during the Mountain Phase of training I became stuck on the side of a mountain. As my strength and the very cold temperatures were about to overpower me, I found the strength to get out of this fix. Earning my Ranger Tab gave my early Army career a kick start. As it turned out, I was never sent to Viet Nam. After a year of serving as a Platoon Leader in the 3$^{rd}$ Armored Cavalry Regiment at Fort Lewis, Washington, I attended Flight Training. So, now I am an Airborne-Ranger-Aviator!

On August 18, 1973, after a very short courtship, I married Joanne. This is the single most significant event of my life. I am convinced that God had a hand in bringing us together-he has saved me a fourth time! I was in Flight School at the time. We would head off to Fort Riley, Kansas for our first year together. Our first daughter would be born at Fort Riley. Following three years at Fort Riley, Kansas - one year in the Republic of Korea and nearly a year at the Armor Officers Advanced Course at Fort Knox, Kentucky - my wife Joanne and I headed to our first tour in the Federal Republic of Germany.

Germany would mark the highlight of my professional career. Along the Frontier of Freedom I commanded a Cobra Platoon in Fulda for one year, followed by command of an Armored Cavalry Troop in Bad Kissingen for two years. The 11$^{th}$ Armored

Cavalry Regiment is the most elite of our heavy units. Our mission was to patrol and defend the East-West German border. These would be the most challenging assignments that I had during my entire Army career.

There is no describing the dedication it took to complete these missions. My soldiers and their families would endure numerous hardships during these years. I would be gone from home over 200 days each year. Joanne deserved medals and bonuses for her dedication and patience. Our second daughter was born in Fulda, only 14 kilometers from the East/West German border. I was a modern day horse-cavalryman.

Returning to the United States in 1982, we headed to Fort Huachuca, Arizona, where I was to attend the Tactical Intelligence Course to prepare me for my next assignment. While there, our third daughter was born. I was not looking forward to this assignment. In those days, officers were required to have a non-combat arms alternate specialty. After much disagreement between me and the Officer Management folks, I chose Tactical Intelligence. Perhaps I could finagle a tour flying twin-engine Mohawks.

After this three-month school, we purchased our first home in Jonesboro, Georgia. I was assigned to the Director of Intelligence, Forces Command Headquarters, Fort McPherson, Georgia. This would be our most stable three years together. I could actually plan to be home for dinner nearly every evening and nearly every weekend. Unfortunately, it was to be my most miserable assignment. I hated

115

every minute of this work. But, even in misery, there were some clouds with silver linings.

One day my boss said that the General was looking for an officer to manage the annual Intelligence Conference. This is the annual meeting of all the Military Intelligence Generals and Colonels in the active Army. Since no one volunteered, I did. This would involve administration, reception, housing, socials, conference, and banquet tasks.

All went well until the steamship round of beef failed to appear as an entrée at the banquet. I took intense heat from the numerous Colonels in attendance. All I could hear up and down the serving line was, "Where's the Beef?" a popular advertising slogan in 1984 from Wendy's! The next day, prior to the wrap up, I visited the Military Police station to borrow riot gear to face the wrath of the visiting officers.

I walked in fully dressed in riot gear to ward off the insults and abuses. Instead, they all laughed their tails off. All was forgiven when I announced that they would receive a $2.00 rebate for the AWOL roast beef! A few weeks later, my general rewarded me with a temporary assignment to Hawaii to evaluate an Attack Helicopter Battalion.

Did this job fit in with my overall plan for success? No! It did not! I would be out of the aviation community main stream for three years. Couple this with my next assignment of another school and I would be out of touch with my peers. This was along with the fast-changing development of Army Aviation's Deep Attack doctrine for a fourth year. This would be the reason that I would not be selected for Battalion Command nor promoted to Colonel.

116

I was able to initiate my Master's Degree in General Business and Management while in the Atlanta area attending an extension of Central Michigan University for four hours every Friday evening and three hours Saturday morning for nearly three years. Unfortunately, the demands of travel would require another year to complete my Masters.

We departed Georgia in 1985 to attend the Command & General Staff College at Ft. Leavenworth, Kansas. This preparatory course for Divisional and Corps-level Staff was the most difficult curriculum of any course I have ever taken or will take. While there, I simultaneously completed my Master's Degree by taking night classes at a Central Michigan extension in Kansas City, Missouri. Needless to say, I couldn't wait to leave Kansas. The good news is that as a result of serving in the 11th ACR and attending C&GSC, I was very competitive for promotion to Lieutenant Colonel.

Next, Joanne, the kids, and I returned to Germany serving as the S-3 Operations Officer, 4th Brigade/1st Armored Division in Katterbach. After three years, we extended our tour for a fourth year and transferred to the 2nd Armored Cavalry Regiment where I served as the Executive Officer (XO) [second in command] of an Air Cavalry Squadron then the XO of the entire Regiment of 3500 men in Nuremberg. Same mission as the 11th Cavalry only now we are within the VII Corp's border sector.

We leased a duplex in a small village called Lehrberg while assigned to the Katterbach unit. We came to know and love the owner of the house and his family. Since retiring from the Army, we have periodically visited each other to this day. My wife

117

and I just returned from a trip to France, Germany and Austria celebrating our 42$^{nd}$ wedding anniversary, which included spending five days at their home in Ansbach. We are, indeed, lifelong friends!

We returned to the States in 1990 just three weeks prior to Sadaam Hussain's attack of Kuwait and the United States' response to the threat. I served as the Deputy Commander of the 6$^{th}$ Cavalry Brigade at Fort Hood, Texas.

The final nail in my career coffin was that this largest attack helicopter brigade in the US Army did not deploy to the Gulf War. As a result, I would trail my contemporaries for promotion who did deploy to the Gulf. In 1993, I went to Fort Worth, Texas for my final year in the US Army in the Airspace Management Office at the Southwest Region of the Federal Aviation Administration.

Upon retiring from the Army after 23 years in 1994, we moved to the Phoenix area. I initially worked for Country Companies Insurance Company. I stayed in this job for approximately 18 months when I moved to McDonald Douglas Helicopter Company. Something was sorely lacking. During this same time, my eldest daughter began college at Texas State University and my middle daughter enrolled in Xavier College Prep. I would discover that this is not the best time to transition from the Army to civilian life.

I earned my Junior Reserve Officers Training Corps (JROTC) Certification prior to leaving the Army just in case I decided to teach at the high school level. During my final week at McDonald-Douglas, I was asked by the Director of Army

Instruction at Phoenix Union High School District to compete for one of its openings. I did and was accepted to teach at Trevor Browne High School. I remained there for two years. I subsequently moved to Marcos de Niza High School in Tempe, Arizona for the 1998-1999 School Year, teaching there for seventeen years.

The mission of JROTC is to help motivate young people to become better Citizens. I could do this. I essentially took over a languishing program transforming it into the finest in the State of Arizona.

JROTC is an elective course. The curriculum has been developed by US Army Cadet Command and is nationally accredited. The program focuses on teaching Citizenship and Leadership. JROTC sponsors extracurricular activities such as Drill Teams, Color Guards, Rifle Teams, Adventure Teams, Saber Teams, and Leadership Academic Bowl teams. I attained my State of Arizona Teaching Certificate.

I immediately pursued a Post-baccalaureate degree at Arizona State University. This is one degree that I would never complete. After earning 30 hours of 4.0 work, I quit with three hours to go because the ASU administrators would not waive my student teaching requirement. At the time, I was teaching high school full time and coaching two teams, one at 6:00 AM and the other at 2:30 PM. When was I supposed to find time to do student teaching?

Looking back, some keys to my success were having two loving parents who raised me in a stable, devoutly Catholic, and safe environment. My parents were fairly strict and, though they didn't demand straight As, they did expect me to work at my very best effort in all things.

Additionally, my father supported my desire to play sports: baseball, football, and track at the expense of working during high school. Instead, he had me work at home as I mentioned previously. I was able to attend and graduate college thanks in great part to my folks. I supplemented their support by working in the dormitory cafeteria and for Illinois Bell Telephone Company. These were terrific experiences. These experiences provided the foundation for my future success.

Joanne sacrificed her life's interests subordinating them in order to support mine, including following me for 23 years in the Army; and another 21 since then. Her support enabled me to focus on the job. Together, we raised three girls, and all graduated from college. I take great pleasure in having Joanne as my wife and companion.

Joanne taught kindergarten for 20 years in the USA and in Germany. I could have done no better. She was acknowledged as an Outstanding Community person by the Commanding General of the 1st Armored Division in Ansbach, Germany. Joanne was named Teacher of the Month by a Phoenix radio station while she taught in the Chandler Unified School District.

My strong faith in God has sustained me throughout my entire life. I remained faithful to Him and planned my weekend around Mass whether it was in a church, on a jeep or Humvee hood, a tank front slope, or on a Cobra wing.

All my experiences leading up to my life as a professional soldier prepared me well: physical fitness, teamwork, strong work ethic, and family love.

Many of the early challenges were the various Army schools, especially Ranger Training. I was only able to complete it thanks to my strong will to never have to tell my father I failed.

I took care of my subordinate officers and enlisted soldiers to the best of my ability. Consequently, when the time came for my soldiers to produce, they always excelled. This principle carried forward following my military retirement and into my next career. I always chose the toughest assignments. These were not only more challenging and gratifying; they usually led to promotions and higher service schooling. Education is always critical. I endeavored to continue to learn. I don't think my Master's Degree had much impact while I was in the Army. But it did contribute to landing the JROTC Senior Army Instructor position.

The US Army Command and Staff College at Fort Leavenworth, Kansas made the most impact upon my career aiding my selection to Lieutenant Colonel and to the Alternate List for Battalion Command.

During my tenure as a JROTC Senior Army Instructor, I worked harder than every other Instructor in the command. I treated my Administrators and Superintendents in education as generals. I would not go home at night without completing a task that my boss assigned me that day. And, I would never allow my Instructors to ever say "No" to anyone asking for help.

I took exceptional care of my subordinate JROTC instructors. I submitted them for awards and recognition multiple times during the year. Each was honored with an award annually. I secured one of them the US Army Cadet Command Instructor of the Year Award. I also kept my fellow instructors better informed than any of my peers. I listened to their concerns, questions, and suggestions. I would implement their ideas whenever it was practicable.

Sustaining my success can be attributed to The Seven Army Values. I believe that a person has to latch on to certain principles in order to have a consistent azimuth for personal growth. The values my parents, teachers, and coaches instilled in me mirror those that the US Army has published - the Seven Army Values:  Loyalty, Duty, Respect, Selfless Service, Honor, Integrity, and Personal Courage. Coupled with the Ten Commandments a person just can't go wrong! I would entwine these with every decision I would make and lesson that I would teach to my students.

I ran 4 miles every other day up to my 44th birthday. Unfortunately, following two orthoscopic surgeries, I had to find other cardiovascular avenues such as walking. Now that I am retired, my wife and I play tennis and swim three to four days per week. Physical fitness promotes mental awareness.

Along with my formal education, I became an avid reader.  Some of my recent reads are:

- *George Washington's Secret Six*: *The Spy Ring That Saved the American Revolution* by Brian Kilmeade
- *The Lion's Gate* by Stephen Pressfield
- *Duty, Secretary of Defense at War*, by Robert Gates

- *Worthy Fights, A Memoir of Leadership*, by Leon Panetta
- *Tell Me How This Ends and the Search for a Way Out of Iraq by* General David Petraeus
- *My Share of the Task*, by Gen Stanley McCrystal
- The ADM William McRaven's commencement address to the graduates of Texas A&M University

My interest in reading began in 8th grade when every evening I watched the Viet Nam war on television. I suppose I wanted to learn more about it since I was convinced I was destined to be sent over there. The earliest book I read that I recall was *Street Without Joy* by Bernard B. Fall.

Later, I was encouraged to study Civil War generals, especially General's Grant and Lee. I read Douglass Southall Freeman's trilogy of *Lee's Lieutenants* while I was on numerous deployments along the East-West German border.

I realized early on that my students were horribly deficient in four critical areas:
- Knowledge of American History - especially Military History
- Writing
- Public Speaking
- Civics

So, in order to improve these deficiencies, I began to purchase, collect, and absorb over 120 books in my personal library. Over time I systematically incorporated the significant campaigns that affected our American historical development into my JROTC Curriculum. The most prominent book we studied was *Killer Angels* by Michael Shaara. My cadets had to read it, were tested on it, and had to make an oral presentation on one day of the battle. Another favorite book key to my instruction of the Mexican War was *Gone For Soldiers* by Jeff Shaara. Perhaps the most comprehensive history collection was Rick Atkinson's *Liberation Trilogy* about our campaigns in North Africa, Italy, and Western Europe in World War II.

To shore up the Civics deficiency, I acquired personal copies of the Declaration of Independence and the US Constitution from the Heritage Foundation. My students would read each in class corresponding to Constitution Day-Sept 17th each year. Now they can say that they read both documents during their high school experience.

I was so disappointed by the Leadership curriculum that the Army provided us that I searched for better books on leadership theory that would be more interesting for my cadets. I found a spectacular book by Jack Uldrich, *Soldier, Statesman, Peacemaker*, *Leadership Lessons from George C. Marshall*. My cadets read the book in class and were tested upon it. Their interest and involvement soared!

I pursued then taught the leadership lessons of the real Titans of World War II: *Masters and Commanders: How Roosevelt, Churchill, Marshall and Alan Brooke Won the War in the West* by Andrew Roberts. Lastly, I found valorous examples of courage and leadership in the Viet Nam War in John C "Doc" Bahnsen's book, *American Warrior*.

124

History will prove that George W. Bush was a great leader. His autobiography, *Decision Points*, is a terrific read about how he led his party and staff with courtesy and compassion. I was very inspired by three books that I have read numerous times over the years:

- *Crossing the Suez* by Gen Shazli
- *The Heights of Courage*, by Gen Avigdor Khalani
- *The Eve of Destruction, The Untold Story of the Yom Kippur War*, by Howard Blum

In order to keep current with our country's events, scandals, and elections over the years I read politically-charged books such as:

- *Culture of Corruption* by Michelle Malkin
- *Clinton Cash* by Peter Schweizer
- *Blood Feud, the Clintons vs the Obamas* by Edward Klein

I have felt the need to familiarize myself with the candidates in the recent elections by reading books by Ted Cruz, Mike Huckabee, Carly Fiorina, and Dr. Ben Carson.

To better understand the current Threat, I sought learned men who could put the Islamist situation into perspective for me. *A Battle for the Soul of Islam*, by Zuhdi Jasser helped me understand the differences between Islam and Islamist. Finally, Lawrence Wright's book, *The Looming Tower* was the definitive exposition for me about Al-Qaeda/Islamic Terrorism.

Considering my spiritual side, I have found Rev Donald H. Calloway's book, *Under the Mantle-*

*Marien Thoughts from a 21st Century Priest* quite inspirational. This has helped me to put all of my past life into perspective by praying to God asking for the intervention of the Blessed Virgin Mary to assist my daily challenges.

Any successes that I have enjoyed over the years were due to my relationships with my parents, teachers, coaches, fellow colleagues, family and friends. Whenever I could I have endeavored to give back of my time, effort, resources, recommendations, and advice to adults and our youth who are facing life's challenges.

I was the Parish Council President in Fulda, Germany. I was a Reader during Mass in Germany, Georgia, and now in Chandler, Arizona. I taught Sunday school to 7th graders in Katterbach, Germany.

I was considered the "Recycle Guy" by my fellow Troop Commanders in Germany because my rehabilitation skills toward young officers who had trouble cutting it as small unit leaders was legendary.

I would never hesitate to give a student a recommendation for a job or a scholarship or application for college entrance, if they deserved it.

I frequently offered to assist fellow JROTC instructors at other schools by sharing my documentation, including Standing Operating Procedures, Information technology, master training plans and teaching procedures, as well on on-site instructional help. I established bi-annual Master Marksmanship Recertification Training for East Valley JROTC Instructors. I sponsored numerous competitive events for the JROTC Rifle Team and the Leadership/Academic Team so students would have game-style competitions.

I established the Program for Accreditation simulated inspection program in preparation for the upcoming visit by our 5th Brigade Headquarters to occur subsequent to my retirement. This will assist the cadets and the Instructors - especially my replacement - in preparing for this newly fielded requirement.

I conducted aviation-related sessions once a month for cadets interested in the aviation industry. And I coordinated bi-annual tours of the TRACON at Sky Harbor International Airport.

I have served 11 years on the St. Juan Diego Capital Campaign Committee to build a second church in South Chandler, set-up/tear-down, ushering and reading during Mass at our temporary site. I am a charter member and Recorder of the newly established Knights of Columbus Council for St. Juan Diego in south Chandler.

I have been a member of the Military Order of the World Wars for 17 years. I have coordinated the joint JROTC and MOWW Remembrance Ceremony every December 7th for the past 17 years. I have forwarded articles and pictures for publication into the "Officer Review" magazine. I sponsored numerous JROTC cadets to the annual Youth Leadership Conference. I have coordinated the annual awards program to 23 ASU ROTC and high school JROTC programs in the Phoenix area. Lastly, I am currently the Senior-Vice Commander.

I actively support the Wounded Warriors, Handicapped Veterans, St. Mary's Food Bank,

Arizona Humane Society, Foundation for the Blind, and the National Children's Cancer Society.

My wife and I attend the annual Blackhorse Association reunions. The Blackhorse Association has provided scholarships to the sons and daughters of fallen Blackhorse Troopers since 1969!

Sustainment of success needs nurturing as well. We all need something to look forward to, something that keeps our minds sharp and is fun. When I retired from the Army in 1994, I never took up golf! Instead, I pursued the attainment of my FAA Single Engine, Instrument, and Multi-engine Instructor ratings. This is the one thing that I indulge myself in from time to time for fun. Some people are terrified of flying; I consider it therapy.

Otherwise, I spend far more time now assisting my daughters and taking care of our six grandkids, ages seven to three weeks whenever I am needed.

Finally, I feel my greatest accomplishment has been my influence and relationship with my wife and my three daughters. Even though the demands of the military and later work required my significant attention, I always placed my family's needs ahead of my own interest. I am gratified that they continue to value my counsel, support, and love to this day.

**Ricardo Blazquez**
**Business Field:** Automotive Executive - Academic
**Business Name:** General Motors - Toyota -
University of Texas El Paso (UTEP)
**Current Position:** Adjunct Professor

**Personal Background:**

First of all please allow me to say this. Many years ago I read the work of Max Depree on Leadership. In one of the chapters there is a piece on "Who made you" and the necessity for reflection on this topic. When I read that, I began to write down information on all the people that have had an impact upon my life. The list began and did not want to end. There are many people to whom I owe an eternal degree of gratitude and to whom I can only repay with the way I try to treat others while trying to help. Therefore, the few people I mention here are a part of so many who helped me in my development, that those who are not mentioned are in no way to be construed as not vital. They are all vital. Those that are not mentioned are eternally in my heart and mind, still working with their ideas and influence. They are the angels in my life.

I was born in Chicago and have 2 sisters, Julia Maria and Anna Maria, and two great parents, Maria and the late Arturo. My ma is from Laredo on the US border and my Father was from Tampico, Mexico. I went to St. Ignatius College Prep in Chicago. St. Ignatius and the Jesuit method of education there had a massive impact on my life. Jesuits teach many ideas but one that I have carried with me "is to see God in all things" and to have the courage to do what is right no matter what the circumstances may be. I played

129

soccer for 4 years. I was a member of their Spiritual Direction Club, which was a program at the school, with a Jesuit by the name of Mark Link S.J.

Father Link has written many books on theology and his ideas inspired a deep sense of respect and tolerance for others in me, as well as the necessity to help others. At lunchtime we would often meet, talk and he would share Mass with me. It was a very wonderful time in my life and a period that I seek to aspire again to be at, as I have drifted from that place. Father Link recently sent me homework that I did when I was in a class with him. This is where I related my struggle and desire to learn to ice skate. I did not give up despite the tears and the freezing. I did not remember it, but it was interesting to read it now. It sounds like what I felt at my best and toughest assignment at GM, Wisconsin-Needmore. He liked it so much that he kept it for almost 40 years! Thank you Father Link! He helped me at GM and beyond.

I was also a student, a volunteer, and eventually a counselor at a place called Midtown, which was a religious boys Center near the Mexican neighborhood of Pilsen in Chicago. It was run by Opus Dei, an order of priests in the Catholic Church who share the same theology as the Jesuits; Catholicism, yet they had a more conservative viewpoint on church teachings. At the time I first went to Midtown, I did not quite understand this, yet while going there after school my Father would often extoll the values of Jesuits and their focus on education and leadership in the spirit of St. Ignatius. I thought that Midtown would be a place to practice this and was simply an extension of Ignatius.

As I began to mature, I began to realize the differences in philosophy of both religious orders; the Jesuits and Opus Dei, and the fact that to me they were a wonderful complement of education, faith, values, discipline, and service to others. During my time at this Center, starting in 6$^{th}$ grade, I was tutored and later on became a tutor. While in high school, I would tutor 6$^{th}$ and 7$^{th}$ graders, and complete other volunteer work there as well. In college I then would tutor high school students. I began to live the cycle of being helped and then helping. I owe much to Midtown for this. I began to hone my sense of leadership there even though I was too young to understand. This note was received from a young man, Albert who I counseled there, and arrived this past December of 2015. It is very revealing to me now after so many years because we all should have "inner voices." We find these in times of deep reflection and as leaders should never give up; especially when it comes to people. Thank you Albert!

*"Rick,*

*Thanks for the articles. Your class syllabus looks very interesting. Every year my goal is to read 2-3 books for my development; I will definitely add the books listed on your syllabus to my 2016 reading list. It is also re-assuring to see you teach this material in hopes of developing future corporate leaders.*

*On a personal note, I'd like to thank you for our years of dialogue and your mentorship. I owe a lot to you. I don't know if you recall back in 1977 during a sports period at Midtown's summer program we had a run in. I guess I had really pushed your last button and you dragged me across Peanut Park and threw me down. You were really pissed at me. You started yelling at me, "Why do you sell yourself short?" and you repeated this several times. My first reaction was why do you give a damn about me; you are not my brother, father or relative. Several days later, the whole incident kept coming back into my mind. I started reflecting upon it and came upon the discovery of what does Rick see in me that I don't see in myself. I had to face the hard reality that I was a quitter and anytime life demanded an effort of me, I would use deflection or sarcasm as a way not to live up to my abilities. As an inner city kid with so many challenges thrown at us, this was a tough lesson to learn and more importantly a tougher character flaw to overcome. Dial it forward, my second week at St. Ignatius; I was pulled out of class by my advisor for our initial introduction only to have her tell me, "I don't see you graduating from here in four years." This really pissed me off and as I walked back to class, I started making excuses for my future failure. As I walked even further, I started hearing in my head, "Why do you sell yourself short?" I committed myself to a new set of study habits, and as you know, graduated from Iggy.*

*After my first quarter at DePaul, I was ready to throw in the towel. College was not cracked up to be all that I thought it was. My first quarter at DePaul, I had received three Bs and one C. I was ready to drop out. However, again I heard that voice*

*in my head, "Why do you sell yourself short?" I
decided to enroll in the winter quarter and apply
myself more diligently. I had developed a set of study
skills that addressed my learning needs and ensured
I was prepared for exams. It literally takes me 8-10
hours to study for a midterm and 12-15 hours for a
final, per subject. I applied myself and received two
As and two Bs. These were the lowest grades I
received for the rest of my undergraduate years.*

*As you said, our upbringing in a Jesuit
education coupled with an Opus Dei formation
compels us to be a different kind of professional. Our
conversation has re-energized me to seek a position
and company whereby I can really contribute and
make a difference the way I know I am capable of
and not to settle for anything less. So when you think
you are not getting through to your students, do not
give up as you just may be changing the trajectory
of someone's life. Thanks for everything and have a
Merry Christmas!"*

All the while at Midtown I was being tutored
as well as receiving spiritual direction. We would
take trips to other Opus Dei centers across the
country and on camping trips. They were lots of fun.
I was with friends, who, like me, wanted to learn,
play sports, and improve. The altar always
accompanied us no matter where we went. One of the
coolest memories of Midtown was having Mass on a
towering sand dune in Michigan while camping
there. Young people like me were together in a very
wonderful place, having a great experience.
Midtown was full of people like me, young Mexican-

American kids from Pilsen, who wanted to study and play sports, as opposed to being in a gang.

Our neighborhood was replete with gangs and I often hear stories about how hard it was to avoid them. I can only say that if gang members saw you walking with books and sports items like a hockey stick or a basketball, they would leave you alone. They knew you had a different set of priorities, including support from parents to that end. Parents are, in my opinion, a very critical foundation. Midtown reinforced in me what my parents, grandmother, grandfather, and Ignatius planted in me, I made good grades in high school, graduated with honors, captained the soccer team, was a member of spiritual direction, and President of the Latin American Students Association.

Right after graduating from high school, I entered DePaul University. One critical element here was that upon graduation from St. Ignatius, I was offered a complete scholarship to my choice of a university stateside. This scholarship was through Dr. Stephen H Fuller from Harvard, who became a mentor to me, while a sophomore at St. Ignatius.

I remember my conversation with Dr. Fuller. I stated that my goal as an undergraduate was to stay in Chicago, complete DePaul in four years, play soccer there, and to work full time as a social worker while in school. This was to help pay off all my tuition, with additional complimentary jobs in the summer, and on weekends. He was very supportive of this as he continued to mentor me. I then received my degree in sociology and history. That was my commitment to myself while executing my original plan.

I also worked while in high school during the summers. This focus on work continued on to college. I would work 2 full-time jobs during the summers while in college. My social work job consisted of working the midnight shift, as it was an emergency program in Chicago. So what I would do in the summer time was get a day-time job, to go along with my night social work job. When I stop to think about what I did in those years, I really don't know how I did it. I was working 40 hours a week on my regular job, then school, and then 16 hours on the weekend at the pizzeria. Summer work during my college years went up to 80 hours a week, plus making pizza on weekends. The real reason for the pizzeria job was to give me some time to hang out with my friends from Midtown, and be in the neighborhood. It was there that I met JoAnn Salas, a young lady who lived near the pizzeria, who I fell in love with. She is a wonderful human being.

During one of my summers in college, when I was looking for a job in the day-time, I was hired by General Motors (GM), in their Electromotive Division. That was the beginning of my life and career at GM. I worked one summer my junior year and made more money than I had ever made in my life. It literally paid for 50% of my tuition from that summer's work at GM. I also was exposed to work in a GM factory and I was attracted to it in a unique way.

My father was an incredibly gifted human being. I say this because he learned to read English by consuming Will and Ariel Durant's, *The Story of Civilization* while using a dictionary to learn words. That copy is one of my most treasured possessions.

He also knew or learned how to do virtually all home and car repairs by himself. This included everything from plumbing to changing an engine. He was a big GM supporter and fan saying that their engines were vastly easier to work on than others. The shop floor at the GM plant and the people there reminded me of my father's garage. I was often times my father's assistant in his work. So, subconsciously maybe GM became an extension of my time helping my father! I never thought about it this way until today.

While I was at the Midtown Boys Club, I found out that one of the benefactors of Midtown was the extended Kennedy Family and friends. I first arrived at Midtown in 1971. The 1960's were a decade of 180 degrees of reality to me. There was great hope and also great tragedy. The underlying factors for both are still being revealed to me today and formed a part of my development in my roles of leadership.

My parents were hard working people who had an affinity to the Democratic Party. My earliest childhood memory was of my parents crying in front of our small TV set when President Kennedy was shot. I became scared and cuddled close to them for not truly understanding the why. A few years later, my father told me that as a Mexican immigrant to the US, who served in our armed forces, he never truly felt that he was a part of our country, until President Kennedy became our leader. He told me that Kennedy and his words were an inspiration to him and helped him feel that he was an American for the first time; no longer marginalized because of his origins or accent. President Kennedy's photo was in our home ever since I can remember.

The Kennedy family's influence was very, very big in Chicago and elsewhere. Our Mayor was Richard Daley, a staunch Kennedy ally, who helped "swing" the election to JFK in 1960. Listening to President Kennedy's speeches and reading about his intentions for our world and its people, was and is both inspiring and insightful to me. In many ways the change he envisioned was courageous, but also radical in the sense that it would change the order of power in the world. It does not surprise me that cowards killed him. In many ways, I feel that he was our last President that tried to do what is right. Corporations and bureaucracies, and the role of true unselfish leadership in them, have many parallels to the reality of President Kennedy and his agenda in terms of politics and one's ability to assess and navigate what can be at times a minefield set by more powerful dimensions. Thoughtful appreciation of this by servant leadership is vital.

One of Midtown's big supporters was a man named Ray Frelk. What I can remember is that Mr. Frelk was a big supporter of the Kennedy family and RFK's run in 1968. As a big supporter of Midtown, he brought a professor from Harvard to Midtown. His name was Dr. Stephen Fuller. I was about 14 or 15 years old when I first met Dr. Fuller. By the grace of God, he became my mentor from that age onward until his passing.

Dr. Fuller, at that time, had moved from Harvard to GM as their Vice-President of Human Relations, on a global basis. Dr. Fuller met a large number of us at the Midtown, but for whatever the reason, Dr. Fuller started to correspond with me. That correspondence with me started what was our process of mentoring. It started when I was 15 and continued for a few years until he passed away. He facilitated the opportunity for me to get interviewed at GM upon graduation from DePaul. I arrived into GM at Fisher Body Livonia as a very green 131 pound front line supervisor. Dr. Fuller then left GM returning to the faculty of Harvard Business School. Dr. Fuller taught Organizational Behavior and related topics. His insights and conviction to the respect of all human beings, especially those with little power, affluence and opportunity, blended very well with what my parents taught me. This was also in line with what the Jesuits and Opus Dei taught me. I would have to say that Dr. Fuller was one of the many "angels in my life."

My very first few moments of introduction at GM Fisher Body Livonia unwittingly taught me very much about my future applied perspectives and actions as a leader in a GM corporate setting. Many of my first introductions at Livonia went like this in varying degrees of time: "Hi, nice to meet you, I'm Joe B., I've got 3 years 5 months and 6 day's to go." I would walk away perplexed by this use of language. I thought then, "Where am I, in a jail?" or reliving a scene "From Each Dawn I Die" with George Raft and James Cagney. Why was it that so many people I met at GM Livonia would end their introductions much like an inmate in jail, with their time left?

Today in the USA according to HBS sources, roughly 43% of Americans go to work unhappy. Therefore, if you are unhappy with something like work, you are just waiting to leave; in short, making an act of presence and not an act of difference! In many ways the ills of GM yesterday and the USA

138

today can be traced to the culture that is built or not built by the leaders of the enterprise and only reflected by the people who comprise them.

If you treat people like objects you are condemned to acts of presence, why should they give anything more? If you fuse people into the body of the enterprise, respecting and creating a system where all their infinite talents can be engaged, you can then expect acts of difference. I also find this phenomenon prevalent in higher education, government, and other sectors. In order to build a system where acts of difference are engaged, leaders must work unselfishly. That should be the rule, not the exception.

Being a product of the 60's and 70's taught me that the struggle for a just world is an essential responsibility of every human, especially those in positions of power and influence. Unfortunately, many of the leaders I met at GM with a few exceptions, like Jerry Elson, Harry Pearce, Mark Weber, Tim Sprecher, Bill Terry, and a few others did not have that connection. It appeared that many only struggled for themselves when they had responsibilities for others and thus society. I was witness to a living aberration of this while at GM-Delphi, in a person who taught me what the anti-thesis of a leader is. In that sense GM, as Dr. Fuller once told me was a great teacher, even if the learning was unpleasant, I still learned.

I saw this more clearly as I was permitted to climb the "ladder" and get to the periphery of their "club"; a place I worked, but a place I knew that I could never completely join or completely be allowed to join. My thoughts and my heart were just

139

not in sync with theirs. Values in GM were clearly stated, I shared them willingly. I eventually learned that as in many organizations, values can be "false monuments" as Nobel Laureate Octavio Paz wrote.

A monument that gives the impression of something noble, when in reality it has no true meaning or reality in society is what I mean. Paz asks us to look at Mexico City as an example of this. A place that is full of monuments to our Native American heritage. When in reality it was Mexico's general and historical treatment of Native Americans. Over time it was shown to be abysmal and cruel. This delusion is not a mental disorder by the government. But a conscious act to appear to be something that it is not. All the while leaders who cross these monuments every day should use their presence and power as leaders as a call to action. It is a call to correct the "falsehood," to rid ourselves of false monuments, and love what they mean.

I eventually learned that many organizations can reflect the shadow of a false monument in varying degrees. The shadows do not conform to the laws of nature. Not for their manifestation, but to the laws and actions of leadership and power who turn values on and off like a light switch instead of letting the sun of values shine 24 hours a day. This degenerates their true essence! There is a tinge of the socio-pathological in this phenomenon. *Living Values* in a company as Herb Kelleher of Southwest Airlines states can truly build an individual psychic satisfaction in the enterprise.

Our job as leaders is to live our values, to serve, and help sustain our fellow workers and their families. It should not be a place to look the other way. Or to obscure and conceal the behavior of a fellow member of the "club," nor a place to line our pockets with golden remuneration or parachutes at the expense of those who are never allowed an opportunity. A sense of societal equity and balance seemed to always be missing in many C- suite dialogues and action, such as past executive compensation at GM, whereas in Toyota it is a bedrock principle. The growth in executive compensation and its disparity today is evident after decades of abuse are indicative of this. A "Gini" like index could be calculated for individual corporations to demonstrate either polarity or equity.

When I think back, I often remember one true anecdote of my life as an executive at GM. I was in charge of Quality for a Division of GM reporting to a President. I was the youngest person on his staff and the most unique from a diversity standpoint. I slowly and gladly evolved into the role of advocate for people who did not look like the executive staff during meetings. That was not a conscious intention of mine as I assumed this role, but one I quickly was thrust into and gladly accepted. As leaders, if something is wrong, something must be done by us.

I was once shocked by the blatant racism once expressed by our Delphi Divisional HR Director about African Americans during a staff meeting. It was a cruel and ignorant statement about his thoughts on the intelligence level of African Americans stated openly at a meeting. I remember that when I heard his remarks, the shock of this bigotry quickly subsided as I countered his ignorance with a clear and forceful revocation. This is now the important part of this lesson to me, as he quickly backtracked on his remarks trying to navigate to a higher ground. But the look on his face to me also intuitively said this, "Ok, Ricardo, with what you just said you confirmed to me that you are part of our staff, but not part of our club." I was not part of the club at GM-Delphi and I am very proud to say so. Last time I checked this man was a CEO of a medium sized company. I only hope that he has changed, but realistically doubt it. Feelings like the ones he expressed reflect a constituent part of his being.

As I worked for this divisional GM President, I was amazed after several staff meetings that many of these high level executives would often sleep or semi-sleep through meetings. Their eyes seemed closed and occasionally would open like a diver coming up for air while swimming. After a few meetings, I observed that this phenomenon seemed to be a learned behavior much akin to a position in yoga yet far more slothful. It was not yoga. It was an act of presence not an act of difference in a boardroom.

It was unbelievable, since they were capable of listening yet were in some kind of somnambulist-like state. For when their names were called or a theme that pertained to their responsibility was brought up, they could quickly and easily open their eyes, then quickly and coherently blend words into the topic at hand; often just connected enough to make some degree of sense and thus reaffirm their position and status in the room. They would then return to this state once the topic that woke them up was contained and another disparate theme was being addressed.

Well, one day, the somnambulists in the executive staff were in full form. When the time arrived on the agenda for a discussion of executive compensation, not only did all their eyes open at once, I never saw 50 something men dive more quickly for their calculators as they quickly began to peck away at them like crazed woodpeckers. They were determining to the "Lord knows what" decimal place what they may be getting that year! This was a GM pathology that I learned from and occasionally teach about today when appropriate. If that energy and focus could only have been directed to the sustainability of people and their communities maybe things would have been different at GM-Delphi; power directed outward to those we serve not to themselves.

I did not live for a bonus. The way I looked at it, if it came it came. It was kind of like manna from heaven. We all were making very good wages that could help a lot of people. The manna could just help a lot more people than me!

Looking back, I graduated in 1981 from DePaul and then went on to GM to work for a couple of years. This was a great experience at GM Livonia. In 1984 I was awarded a Sloan Fellowship. Then I was accepted and received full fellowship opportunities from Harvard, University of Chicago, University of Michigan, Wharton School of Business, and at Northwestern (Kellogg). Since it was a Sloan Fellowship, I could pick where I wanted to go to school. I chose Northwestern.

There were 3 teachers who had a massive impact upon me at DePaul. Dr. Bernadine Pietraszek in History made caring and learning so much fun. I will always remember her kindness, humanity and intellect. Dr. Deena Weinstein and her husband, the late Michael Weinstein, were very instrumental, not only in my development as a student but in my post graduate days as an executive. Brilliance is the only word to describe them. The light that they so kindly gave to me still shines around me today. Their books, humane thoughts, and spirit have accompanied me around the world. They have helped guide me through some very challenging issues.

After I graduated from Northwestern, I went back to GM's Fisher-Body plant in Livonia, Michigan. When I went back into the plant, I went in as a General Supervisor. I think the success that we had in this plant assignment, was due to the people that worked with me. This included the experience and success they had. I learned a lot from them, as they all had 25-30 years of experience.

I was 26 years old. I could be their son. When speaking with them, I addressed them formally as I was taught by my parents. This was not common at GM. I would call them Mr. Gensen, Mr. Smith, Mr. Baranski, etc. I did not refer to them by their first names. That created an atmosphere that was a little unique on the shop floor, where formal respect was tangible, at least in the atmosphere that I attempted to establish. When I worked there, it was in a place where there was often a lack of respect between the workers and the supervisors, where survival meant navigating often very cruel and at times inhumane corners. I always sought to establish this atmosphere of respect, where I worked independently of the ridicule that sometimes came my way. The line workers were never a source of ridicule, which came from management. This shaped me. This reality is what I wanted to help change when and if I could.

About 6 months into my assignment at GM Livonia, I was asked by one of the workers at the plant who did not directly work for me if I would like a home cooked meal. Mr. Michael Genson knew that I was alone in Detroit away from my family. I went to his home and met his family and ate a very good meal prepared by Mrs. Genson. Forty plus years later, both Mr. and Mrs. Genson are still a second set of parents to me. Their love and gifts to me are infinitely wonderful and can never be repaid. They have taught me so very much, most of all a lesson in love. After about 10 years of knowing Mr. Genson and sharing so many wonderful times and anecdotes about plant life at GM and the people and characters there, he developed a brain tumor. He left for surgery to the Mayo Clinic. I was very frightened for him and wrote a note to him while he was prepping for surgery there.

I essentially told him that I loved him and wished him the very best and that I prayed for his quick recovery. Why did I write him to tell him that I loved him as a second Father? Why did I wait until he had a tumor and was ready to be operated on? The lesson Mr. and Mrs. Genson taught me was to never wait to tell someone that you love them; life is full of moments to do this with words and with actions-just do it. Do not wait for death to express love. A lesson that is deeply in my heart just like Mr. and Mrs. Genson.

I also always used my name Ricardo on my name tag at GM. In spite of my friends in Chicago calling me Rick or Ricky I always kept it as Ricardo.

I was proud of my name and my heritage. This often became a source of ridicule in some quarters of GM. My identity was always clear to me and I carried it with me quietly to others.

I was then promoted from General Supervisor to Superintendent in Materials. After that, I was promoted to Quality Director. The Quality Director role propelled me into a role of a "Baby Plant Manager" of a small facility in Michigan. It was a test. This was a Plant Manager's job in Auburn Hills, which was a seat assembly plant. I was there for about 14 months. It was kind of a unique assignment because it only had 300 people. It also allowed me to operate in a very independent way and to help work in a team. I was blessed with wonderful team members and a wonderful staff. Ed DeRosa, Paul Piccio, Don Sykes (All-American from West Point), Clennie Brundidge, former Detroit Tiger Mitch Monzcka, and Boyd Tindell. All of us along with Lisa, Wes, Sam, and others created a deep sense of family at that plant. We shared leadership, did some very creative things, and cared for people and our customers. I loved Auburn Hills.

When I got there, I found that the Plant Manager's Office was a massive office, private bath, and a small wet bar. That was "offensive" to me. Since I felt that way, I immediately converted it into a team room for the workers to meet and plan improvements. This is when I began to tinker with *Lincoln on Leadership*. Also at this time, I started looking at things from a Quality perspective, as well as the Toyota Production System (TPS).

At this time, these concepts were somewhat different, when you think about manufacturing and the management of a manufacturing plant. This was the time that GM played host to literally bashing Toyota cars in parking lots as a pseudo sport. When visiting Buick City in Flint, one would find in the lobby of one of their buildings, the image of an Asian person with the words "Our Enemy" underneath it. Beyond the disrespect, I felt that if there was an enemy, it was the people who put such a pathological display on in the first place.

Flint and GM Flint-GMI was a place where incest took place at GM in a philosophical and cultural sense. The inbreeding of ideas and future leaders was in many ways given life in Flint. Although the educational and professional experiences there did produce a few open minds at GM, it was not enough to turn the tide for meaningful change. Like the RFK book *The Enemy Within*, Flint and its often times narrow philosophy and worldview, had a way of permeating GM and its leadership for decades, even up to this day.

At Auburn Hills, Industrial Relations along with the UAW, was a most unique lesson and experience, even though Quality and Team Building were very close. We attempted to build a family-like atmosphere, where safety of the employee and service to the customer were our major priorities. We did this with people. People at a traditional GM plant are typically the sole purview of the UAW. This can be understood historically; by the way workers have generally been treated by management at GM from its inception. It is far better today than at its origins, although there are still many gaps. We tried to build a spirit of "We" at Auburn Hills, not the typical "Us"

(Management) vs. them (UAW). This change ruffled some traditional feathers.

We had a Shop Chairman who was very traditional in his principles. Glen loved to chew tobacco. He would hold a cup in his hand, and then spit into the cup, as he was talking to you. I am glad he had perfect aim! Glen thought that tradition should continue to govern the relationship in the plant. The "We" was somewhat unconventional. In retrospect the "We" would precipitate the loss of some of his traditional power over the rank and file.

I remember that he called for a strike vote about 10 months into my time there and 10 months into the "We." This is significant because I think that this was the first time in history the following had happened at a GM plant, or at least had been disclosed to the light of day. He called for the strike vote on some charges in the area of safety issues in the cafeteria. So Glen took the authorization for the strike vote and the workers proceeded to vote. At this time, I thought that my career was over at GM. Tim Sprecher, the GM Assembly Plant Manager across the street from Auburn Hills and our sole customer was a mentor and teacher who supported me during this time with wise counsel and feedback.

As the strike vote arrived, I figured that this was it! On a personal level I was very sad. I knew the real reason behind the vote, was the atmosphere that we began to build with everyone being like a family. This was something that was threatening to both traditional forms of union-management relations. My first job as a plant manager and a strike vote being called! I better find another job. But what happened was shocking or maybe not so shocking.

As the strike vote day passed, I was sitting with Don Sykes, our exceptional HR Director, a true gentleman and professional waiting for the results to be announced to us. I was not aware of the formal protocol of a strike vote at the Union Hall. All I knew was that if the workers supported the strike, it would then go to the UAW National Headquarters for their consideration and potential support. If received there, and if affirmed by the national parties, then the plant workforce could go out on strike.

We built seats for 900-1000 vehicles a day for our customer, the GM Orion Plant. A strike would idle them and countless suppliers and workers. All this was over a rather capricious belief on the part of Glen. The afternoon passed. It was about 7 pm when Don received a call from one of our line workers by the name of Stan. I was in the office. Stan told Don that a group of workers went to the Union Hall, at the conclusion of voting, and demanded that the votes be counted in front of them. Glen told them that an "election committee" would count the votes, sanction the results, and that the group of workers could leave. Stan, Wes, and others stayed and demanded, using what I was told, some very creative means to force the opening of the box by Glen and a count of the vote right then and there with them as witnesses. As the workers were present for the vote count, they wanted Glen to sign-off on the actual numbers of *yes* and *no strike votes*. Then they wanted the vote results to be formally announced. The workers voted against the strike approximately 80% to 20%.

Don got off the phone and had a look of disbelief on his face, yet I could tell he was so happy.

149

He called our GM headquarters with the news. We then began to receive many calls from the GM building on this result. After a few minutes Don told me that this had never happened before in the history of GM, that is, a strike vote called by the local UAW shop chairman being turned down by the rank and file members. Now many years later, I do not believe this to be the case. Maybe it was the first time that workers demanded votes to be counted in public view, not behind the closed doors of an "election committee." This event was reflective of the unity we built at this plant among all of us, not any one person. It did however follow me at GM.

Since I was still rather young and still somewhat inexperienced, I did not know or fully comprehend the impact of what happened. As days passed, we started getting phone calls from GM's 14th Floor (C-Suite). This was along with visits to our plant by GM Leaders. It really dawned on me that we were on to something so very simple, but unfortunately so poorly practiced at times by GM Management. It was simply respect and being true to your team members, by supporting them on the shop floor, with them in their daily struggles, trying to make their work lives better. I felt for the first time a sense of community and love for one another in a plant. I know some may contest these words and they have that right, but we did have this at Auburn Hills. I cried privately when I moved to another assignment. They are all in my heart and that is still a blessing.

So in the end that whole incident gave me a "tattoo" of sorts. This tattoo, never told to me directly, but intuitively sensed by me. It was that GM thought that Ricardo could get along with UAW workers. I thought and think, why not? In fact, I generally felt better among UAW workers than anyplace else while at GM. I did and still do respect and enjoy many salaried and executive friends. But in the end, I was attracted to support those with the least power and with the greatest needs. This included many salaried people, but again the vast majority was workers no matter where I was located. I feel that it is far more natural and human to help someone in need with limited power than someone who makes 6 figures and with some degree of power although if with need I would help.

This became a big part of my life because at that point in time, people from GM started coming to the plant. They were asking questions about what had happened and how did I get the results that I did on the vote. I did not, the people did. Respect for people did. Focus on the Customer did. All that you give to others, you give to yourself. The golden rule is an essential tool for managers and leaders.

As I reflect upon the essence of what we did at Auburn Hills, it really was no more than a primitive version of the Toyota Production System (TPS). What it is, is a whole lot of respect and support for the workers on the floor. It was the "openness" that we had in the plant to discuss issues and get resolutions together. What we really had was a great, great team of people in the plant. A system to direct all our collective talents was initially built.

After this, I was sent to Mexico for the first time. My assignment was to be the Operation's Manager of Fisher-Body facilities in Mexico, along our southwestern border. I was in the position for about a year and then I became the Managing Director of the Operations. I learned to respect the necessity for deep systems from my initial supervisor on this assignment. It was Mr. DeFalco, a most cerebral and well-read person. This assignment included about 8 facilities in Mexico and a joint venture with a ruthless partner in Mexico. This person was a living example of all elements of a human being that are repulsive to me. He represented another process of learning for me, albeit at times toxic.

Also at that time, GM was in the process of closing a plant in Van Nuys, California. The remnants of the Van Nuys facility fell under my responsibility. What I did at that location, was to assist in the transition of employees at that location to other facilities within GM. Many of the people went to New United Motors Manufacturing (NUMMI) plant, which was a joint-venture between Toyota and GM. Also during this time, I went to NUMMI for training and to MIT for the "Leaders in Manufacturing" program.

Mexico was and is special to me, since my ancestors are from there. I spent several summers on the gulf coast with my grandmother, her mom, my great grandmother, and her sister-my great aunt, when I was very young. They each were loving and great teachers to me. At this time, Mexican GM plants were generally managed by non- Mexican executives.

I was very grateful to Mr. DeFalco, who built a solid foundation of systems at these plants. I solely tried to improve our performance while also deeply attempting to embed respect for workers in Mexico.

All our plants in Mexico were non-union, the last GM plants in this category. I felt a responsibility to be the union for our team members, in a way their advocate. We began to apply a deeper system for human engagement in these facilities with the support of many wonderful people. Our metrics were some of the best in GM and our process of continuous improvement was solid in all major categories.

We built a museum of Mexican Archaeological Culture at our main plant. This was the headquarters for our team members and their families. This, along with great support from Mr. Jerry Elson, a GM Divisional President and a great human being, made our work in Mexico very enriching. It included respect for workers and their families. This was a preeminent factor in our management philosophy. Having a superior like Mr. Elson, who expected results with respect, was great! Yet, every coin has two sides and you learn lessons from both. Prior to my tenure as Managing Director in Mexico, a Joint Venture (JV) was established between our unit, and a company run by a Mexican millionaire in Mexico City.

As I transitioned to my new role, I received a call from Mr. Elson asking me to assess the state of this JV. It seems that the JV, which supplied the GM assembly facility in Mexico City, was performing very badly. It was unable to keep up with production, thus not sending complete seat sets to the assembly plant, and leading to the accumulation of nearly 2000 vehicles with incomplete interiors. I was asked to go there on a Saturday and make a recommendation as to whether we get out of the venture or stay in. I arrived on a Saturday and began to walk the facility. It was the worst plant I had ever seen in terms of raw management and wasteful flow. I soon determined the source of the waste. This JV confirmed what Dr. Deming often alluded to in terms of management being the ultimate source of dissonance in the enterprise and not the people. The plant belonged to a millionaire who I will refer to as M in the 26 million megalopolis of Mexico City.

I was asked by my superiors in Detroit to reply back to them upon arrival in Mexico City with my initial impressions of the facility. Further, I was asked whether I thought that we could "make" production or not. It was essentially in my hands as to whether we dissolved the JV or not. I walked in the plant and avoided blocked aisles and various production anomalies that Saturday morning. All the while a crew worked to produce seats for the Chevy Suburban production in Mexico. I was aware of the huge deficiency in production that resulted in semi-produced vehicles sitting in rented lots across Mexico City. This was a result of management ineptitude. This was called putting vehicles in the yard as they could not be shipped.

As I walked the plant with M, I could not help but look at the workers, the people in this plant and their faces. I saw faces of humility and hard work, part of my culture as working class people. They did not want to look my way as I walked with M. It became very apparent to me that M knew very little about manufacturing, thus leaving it to others to run this business, but he definitely set a tone of fear and intimidation. This became very evident in the plant as people began to refer to him as "patron." This is a term prevalent in pre-revolutionary Mexico that referred to the ruling classes. This was primarily in many cases to the owners of haciendas and big chunks of land by their workers. It is a term that subjugates the actual person who uses it, in the eyes of the person he is addressing with it. Never in my life, had I heard it used as I did on that tour, in open reference to M, by all segments of workers.

As I asked questions of M, he would often turn to a person following us for the answer. This was November, right before the holidays. I could see the reason for worry in Detroit. We left the JV in the hands of people who had very little in common with us, in terms of values and operational acumen. I asked M where the cafeteria was located as he walked in the direction of an exit. He then walked out the door to the street, where various vendors had set up small humble food stands. He snapped his fingers like a singer and pointed to the curb on the sidewalk. He did it twice as if to reinforce the inhumanity of his response to me. He sickened me to my stomach with what he did, yet my reaction was muted to him. I just took it all in, like everything else on the tour.

I knew this was going to be a hell of a job to turn around, with very little time to do it. I also knew that M had to get out of the way in order to turn this place around. We would have to do it our way. A human way that was readily taught to me by people like Bill Terry, Larry Kesler, Jerry Elson and Mancel Cooper at GM. Preeminent in my mind were the workers and their lives and families. I sincerely mean this. This was at the core of what I ultimately chose to do. In Mexico by law, workers receive literally double pay for Christmas, and this was just around

155

the corner. I had to judge M that day, along with his ego and potential motivations. This was just in case we pulled out of the JV.

I had to determine the impact of a decision like this and its impact upon people. I chose to find a way to fix this and win for our customer and workers. I called Detroit and notified them of my decision. When I did this I had no formal plan other than my word that we could do it. I thought with my heart that day, something that this true story proves you can do. My only plan was to lead this effort with a team of great leaders from our GM operations in Mexico. But the "How" was missing. Yet again a lesson was in the making for me here. Great people and great teams find a way!

I was given permission to bring in our "A" team of Salvador, Silvia, Ruben, Jaime, Rosy, Cesar, and Emilia. They began to arrive Sunday. I did not leave the plant for 82 consecutive hours. I survived on the spirit of all these great workers, the "A" team, their leadership, cookies, and juice. We began to adjust the flow of the process with the help of the workers starting on Saturday. By Monday morning we were ready to go live with the customer. We met the schedule for the first time ever and did not put any vehicles in the yard! Zero! Tuesday morning I left to rest at the hotel and was back the following day with the Team.

This "A" team worked from 0600 to 2200 every day for about 6 weeks. The curiosity of our hotel hosts at the Maria Christina were mystified with the hours we led. One of their managers after weeks of seeing us work this way asked us what we did. Ruben answered simply, "We help people build

156

cars for customers." As we gradually began to produce more than we needed, thus reducing the size of the vehicles in the yard, the pressure dropped and the building of a system with people could take hold for higher levels of achievement. To this end, we also began to build a system based on respect and inclusion of team members. M stayed out of the way!

Emilia worked to dignify the conditions of the workers in the plant, including free meals, decent places to eat, and the conditions of the bathrooms. This is one last point to me about the JV in the first place. It was brokered by people in GM with either a blind eye to the values of M or with similar pathological values. How can this happen to GM? I have reflected on this for years and with years comes at least some answers and speculation.

I keep learning as I look at what happened to American GM-Delphi workers recently and one can see parallels in this type of abusive mindset. Executives, who are so far from the struggles and suffering of working class people and very close, too close to hedge fund managers suffer from self-inflicted and purposeful blindness. This is what Robert Reich and Paul Krugman write about today, essentially the wealth of poverty, and the poverty of wealth in our world. Socio-pathology of the first order is a rampant disease in many market-based enterprises emanating from the more viral attributes of Wall Street where hubris displaces humility and self-aggrandizement dislodges humanness.

Allow me one last anecdote about M and his poverty of wealth and its manifest nature. Prior to our arrival, M instructed his leaders to hand out to all workers, their monthly supply of toilet paper on a

Popsicle stick. Yes, I know this is hard to believe, but this is true. M and his leaders would take the time to roll out about a quarter of an inch of paper on a stick and give it to workers once a month. There was no toilet paper in the bathrooms and you can just imagine their state. At the time, the President of Mexico was a man by the name of Gortari.

This only augmented my plans and desire, to put a huge effort into upgrading bathrooms and doing away with the Popsicle stick. I called the effort the "Gortari" bathrooms, a place where even the president of Mexico could someday sit, meet, and possibly even eat. With intended irony, I actually did this on a couple of occasions, calling meetings there with M where he was offered a small cup of coffee while watching workers arrive for biological reasons. This is where I would discuss issues, since I was given authority over the entire JV. I could do it my way. This was one of the only times that the power I had was consciously used and planned for. I loved the meetings there with M, accomplishing much beyond the essence of the business issues at hand! It taught M nothing but exposed him to everything if you know what I mean, because he remained the M, the Popsicle man. But as I tried to humanize him and his patron, like an aura among all classes of the workers, I instantaneously realized that this was a task only worthy to the ancient Greek, Sisyphus. Therefore, doing it was more important than the results. Workers saw the impossibility of conversion yet were glad that M could be forced to come back to the planet Earth. Hopefully, it is something that he can remember from time to time. This would be a wonderful result, albeit temporal!

In addition, the workers could visualize the lesson I attempted to teach in human respect. That is in spite of their past humiliations, there could be an equal playing field, albeit for a short period, where the hubris of misguided leadership and power could feel and see another way. I was very proud to be part of GM and working for a person like Mr. Elson, who would support me in this endeavor.

When I made Managing Director in Mexico, Dr. Fuller had already left GM and returned to Harvard. We would sit back and talk about the things that I did and the movement that I had made while at GM. He, as well as my father, always emphasized people, respect, and the pursuit of personal excellence, knowledge, work, and family in my varied interactions with them. I remember, that in my career, I never resurrected Dr. Fuller's name once.

Only about 3-4 years ago would I begin to talk about him openly. The big influence on me was that he would talk about the traditional mode of operations that existed in GM factories. We also discussed the abnormal relationships that existed between people in the plants. The abnormal had become normal in so many places at GM. I learned this phrase from a janitor at GM's Wisconsin-Needmore complex of plants.

But, we also talked about the good things that went on at the GM plants. He once said that one of the best things about GM is that it is just a huge laboratory for learning about human interaction. About 90% of the learning that I had at GM was not from my executive leadership, but from the people. If I look at my overall learning, it has been 90% from GM and 10% from Toyota. Of the 90 % at GM, it was from rank and file, then 10% from some very special executives. From GM, Jerry Elson and Dr. Fuller are at the top of this list. The depth of the 10% from Toyota accounts for 80% of my viewpoints on how enterprises should be run.

After my assignment in Mexico, I ended up in my "dream assignment." This assignment was at the Wisconsin-Needmore Rd. Plant in Dayton, Ohio. Initially, when I was told I was going to Wisconsin-Needmore, I thought that I was going back to Chicago. I really didn't know what Wisconsin-Needmore was at that time. At the end of July in 1996, the GM Wisconsin-Needmore Plants in southern Ohio and GM had just called a "cease fire" in a one month strike that had virtually shut GM North America and its entire value stream down. Tensions and fear were high at GM and the UAW corridors as the industry and the nation slowly recovered and people came back to work. This was the place and the circumstances I was asked to lead. I arrived from my assignment in Mexico the day after the cease-fire was called and operations had resumed. I owe Mr. Mark Weber from GM much gratitude for his preemptive faith in me, and the gift of the very toughest, and yet best assignment in my life.

I think that I was picked to go to Wisconsin-Needmore because of the profile that I had established in Auburn Hills. This was working with people and the team atmosphere that we established with a customer focus. I think that GM had realized and connected the fact that I try to work well with all people, often times breaking down barriers.

This would include the use and terminology of hourly and salary people at GM. From day one at GM these terms were so foreign to me. They were only words and labels and yet at times powerful and harmful barriers in a world already full of natural ones. We need not create human forms to augment the natural ones. Their destructive derivatives continue to evolve to this day in many organizations.

Bill Terry, a great plant manager at GM, taught me many lessons. One I shall never forget. I would often work very late at Livonia. One day on second shift during the dinner break Mr. Terry called and asked me to take a walk with him. We walked through the plant just looking, ending up at the cafeteria. As we stood looking at this huge room with about 150 full tables in it, Mr. Terry asked me how many groups of people I could see. I answered one. He asked that I look again. I repeated my answer and he said that we as a plant had a long way to go until we were unified. He said, "Ricardo, look white supervisors with white supervisors, blacks with blacks, and so on." He said with his confident and sincere smile. "We have a long way to go, but we will do it." Bill Terry taught me that leaders have a unique role to play in building bridges. If leaders accept it, the role will take on what at times can be a very arduous but necessary task.

The way I look at it, God has created enough barriers in the world, why do we as humans feel compelled to keep building more; union/salary/white/black. We are on this tiny planet for a reason, to be together, and live together. I just really wanted to put this into practice as I worked for what I truly believed in a hierarchal organization. We are only as great as the least among us. Therefore support for the most humble of workers is where an enterprise system must begin. Do not ask a CEO if his or her company is great. Ask the most humble person in their hierarchy and if the answer is an unbiased yes, then take it to the bank! Answers to that question as you get closer to the top of an organization have a tendency to lose a bit of accuracy unless their foundation is in the most humble of its workers.

Servant leadership is often in vogue in executive circles. However, unless its source can be traced in an auditable form to the worker, it is meaningless and often simply a false monument. Unfortunately, false monuments often predominate the business landscape. Ask the retired salaried workforce at Delphi prior to the bankruptcy about how great their firm was.

This is what I feel is so compelling about business. It is what the leaders can do in the world beyond the product or service. It goes beyond the cash flow and the income statement. Businesses can do such good for people and our communities. With the power and influence we possess, we can help change what we encounter and what requires change and attempt to make the world we touch a better place.

As leaders we can never lose sight or become blind to the ancillary good that we can do. The desperate state of our world deeply needs support on so many fronts. It is a wealth of poverty and a poverty of wealth. I just read that every 4.2 seconds a child on our planet dies because of the lack of clean water. Deep, meaningful change can be driven from the corporate suites beyond the superficial optics of United Way drives! Today this ideal is what drives my instruction in my classes while I tried very hard to do this in my roles in the private sector. I share these ideas with young MBA students at UTEP, our future leaders, which gives me great hope as it can and will be better!

At Toyota, management is taught by a simple question when interacting with workers. "How can I support you?" It really all starts there with a system based on people. Organizations produce value or utility with simply people's capabilities and strategy. Management conducts this process. Hopefully with humanity and a rhythm of an operating system for societal benefit, there can be sustainability of those who comprise this team and beyond. By building a place where a team can use tools in a system, that produces deep knowledge and shared learning, an enterprise philosophy is lived, and a culture created. It can also be reinforced which can lead to a deep sense of value that has many dimensions.

People and respect for them is the essential building block. My opinion has many sources going back to my social work days, my Jesuit education, my grandparents and parents. It goes back to the mentorship that I had received from Dr. Fuller. When he and I would talk, we would be in discussions about how humans behaved. I would say that Dr. Fuller had a deep, deep commitment to society, humanity, respect, inclusion, and sustainability. My grandparents and parents shared the same lessons in deep cultural ways.

As a child, my parents would send me, Anna and Julia, my sisters, to my paternal grandmother's home, by way of my grandfather's Jesus' maternal home in Laredo, Texas. It was literally our last stop in the United States prior to heading to Tampico on the coast of Mexico. We would spend the summer with my grandmother Maria, her mother Trinidad and her sister my great Aunt Aurelia. The love that was extended to us was infinite. The lessons from each of them were simple, yet deep with meaning. Family, respect, work, and sacrifice were in constant reflection to each of us. Without these lessons my work would be diminished greatly.

My grandfather lost his wife Juanita, giving birth to their eighth child. He raised their 8 children with the help of his cousin, all the while working the fields of south Texas, and making seasonal treks to the north. He had more dignity in his finger than a thousand "Ms!" Quiet and stoic, I interviewed him, and have his recording on tape. It is very hard to listen to his quiet words and leadership without crying. I miss him. He helped to make me who I am, how I work, and how I work with people.

My grandmother's home in Tampico sat on a street of sand, not too far from the beach. Most of the streets at that time were not paved, but had varying degrees of rocks and pebbles in them. Next door lived my father's first cousin, my uncle in Mexican culture, Ricardo and his sister Dolores, and not too far away his brother Adolfo, also my aunt and uncle. We were surrounded by a community of many other children, playing and learning all day long. Deep learning of Spanish took place while having fun and being loved, while also getting a strong dose of Mexican culture.

My family was not rich by typical economic standards, yet the values and culture they shared could run a Fortune 25 company extremely well! My grandmother's kitchen was in the middle of a garden that was replete with many trees that bore fruit. There were Mangos, papayas, peaches, apricots, avocados, oranges, limes, coconuts, and tamarinds. It was a small kitchen with gas tanks propelling the stove, and a dirt floor. Every morning the windows made of wood, not glass would be swung open and the day would begin there, and end there with dinner.

We would often accompany my grandmother to the open air market about 4 blocks away. We would be greeting neighbors along the way and interacting with strangers who were greeted with respect and reverence. Interacting with the vendors for the day's essentials was also conducted with great dignity, as my grandmother had her favorite vendors.

My grandmother, great grandmother, and great aunt were all very special. They were people who gave, with nothing expected in return. It was a unique form of love. One day while sitting in the kitchen, my grandmother noticed a man sitting just outside our cyclone fence on a bench, under the shade of the tamarind tree. My grandmother had the bench built because as she told me, many people would walk past our home, from either work or the central market in the stifling heat of the day, and need a place to rest in the shade. We had already eaten breakfast and my grandmother began to quickly prepare another plate of food and began to warm some tortillas. I found this odd.

She then asked me to take the plate of food, a few tortillas on top, along with a lemonade to the man who was sitting on the bench, who was an older gentleman. I was about 6, and I was afraid to do this. Yet trusting my grandmother, I did not let fear manifest in my heart. It started with my slow steps to the front of the house, on through the front gate, slowly extending the plate to the stranger. I looked at his parched face and straw hat as a fellow human being, not a stranger. We spoke no words as his hands reached out and took the plate. I ran to get the lemonade and the ritual repeated itself.

As I returned inside the gate and fence, I sat on the ground just inside the cyclone fence and watched the man eat. My curiosity was childlike as I looked and marveled at him roll and use the tortillas. He used both utensils and food as he cleaned the plate. As he concluded, he rose and approached the fence handing both plate and glass over the fence saying gracias. Since then, I have never feared "giving" to a fellow human being, even a stranger, while addressing an issue. No MBA class could teach this lesson as well as Grandma Maria taught me in 10 minutes

I have said all of this to try to explain, why I have done things in a certain manner in my career. My experiences in my life have contributed to my behavior in my career. Formal education can teach you much. Informal education can teach as much, or in my opinion, even more.

The late Mancel Cooper was a person who taught me very much about learning in informal settings, such as the plant floor. I consider Mancel an older brother that I never had but did when he came into my life. I first met Mancel at GM Livonia, where his common sense approach to management and people could reduce complex issues in quality, management, and labor relations to a fine point. He was a master of getting to the heart of the matter and cutting away distractions and rhetoric.

A former Army veteran who guarded the body of President Kennedy prior to events at Bethesda, Mr. Cooper taught me many lessons, but one that is very critical. In order to take on great challenges, be a part of a great team. This is all the more important at critical times. All members of a team support and have roles to play, but what many teams lack is a system to perform day in and day out. Identify the system, use it, improve it day to day, and the challenges that one may deem difficult can be overcome. Mr. Cooper taught me so much about management, but also about the sensitive issues of race as it pertains to African American people in the GM system. We shared tears and much laughter and he helped me deeply become who I am today.

During my assignment at Wisconsin-Needmore (WN), Joe B. the Shop Chair and I would conduct all-employee meetings on a monthly basis. This was done with the help of wonderful people like Jim, Barb, Rich, Mahlon, Tony, Julie, Mark, and so many others. Without their help, we would be unable to do this. On one occasion I wanted to hand out some cards that I had made up and laminated called the Leadership Cards. Being two sided they were based on the Lincoln Leadership Principles and some of his ideas on the subject of leadership. I did this to try to instill in all our plant personnel, where I was coming from as a plant manager.

Joe was the leader of the month-long strike against GM prior to my arrival. When I first met him,

I immediately liked him a great deal and respected him. I feel Joe was incredibly misunderstood by GM. He was a person whose outward appearance was strong in virtually every way. But he was a leader and deep inside he was a human like all of us. He had convictions and was a repository of lessons for any PhD teaching labor relations. In certain corridors at GM, his humanness was either ignored, or little effort was taken to understand it. This alienation in turn precipitated and helped to form Joe, his leadership, and his viewpoints. He was elected to lead the UAW at these plants and lead the 4500+ UAW members and people.

Prior to the all-employee meetings, Joe and I would review what was to be shared and then proceed. The meetings consisted of key metrics we developed and shared (40% of the time) and open questions (60% of the time). We had good energy together and demonstrated by our joint presence a commitment to act as a team, something very unique in the plants' histories. This was so vital in light of our past at these plants where division among people, union, and management was so prevalent. One of my earliest gifts to the joint leadership team (union and management leaders) at WN was a laminated card that I had compiled while at Auburn Hills. It is the Lincoln and Leadership Card, a series of principles of leadership that reflect the style of our 16th President.

I asked Joe if I could give a copy of the cards to all of the workers. He hesitated and said something to the effect that the cards were on leadership. I sensed a small degree of reluctance and then I shared with Joe that I thought that all people could be leaders, if given the opportunity. I envisioned a culture where people, when seeing a problem or an issue, could feel the freedom to do something about it. Given this philosophy, that we all could be leaders, he allowed me to pass out the cards to the entire membership. This was just like my grandmother had demonstrated to me with the man on the bench. She did something about his hunger! Knowledge, like food, can feed human beings. We can all be leaders when we see something that is wrong.

Wisconsin-Needmore, like Joe, was misunderstood by GM. Traditional management-union adversarial roles were an art form there. It was a surreal scene founded on lack of respect. Without respect and the demonstration of ancillary virtues, progress on most issues, would remain in a state of deep freeze while the world passed us up. The resolution of the plants' issues would become more complex as a function of time. Upon arrival at Wisconsin-Needmore, I was told by my management to tell the "people" there, that either we would "fix, sell, or close" the plants. This was an in vogue "Welchism" (Jack Welch-GE) used in corporate circles at the time.

This is not the textbook kind of greeting that I, as a new Leader of 7 unique plants, at two locations, about ten miles apart should begin his tenure with. I made the decision to meet first with the Union Leadership. Jim set up the meeting. This was my first full day. The process that we used was called a New Manager Assimilation.

There were about 35-40 Union leaders of Wisconsin-Needmore in the room. I was introduced to the entire team. After some perfunctory remarks

169

that lasted no more than a minute about being a pleasure to be there, I asked them if they had any questions.

After a few seconds, they asked if I could leave as they formulated questions for me. I agreed and left with Jim, Mark, and other members of management. Upon returning a few minutes later, I began to address questions.

The first question was, "How long did it take me to get to Dayton from Mexico by donkey?" I answered in a very calm tone, "Ladies and gentlemen, I believe the major issue we face here is the amount of money, we as an enterprise lose in one day. Roughly 1 million dollars a day and that I look forward to working with you on this!" The second question was, "Did you buy a home here with a barn for all of your donkeys?" I answered this question the same as the first, with a focus on the Customers who were impacted from our strike, and the fact that we had much work to regain their support and trust. The third question continued with a question that culminated with cruel disrespect to my extended family. I answered this question in the same way that I answered the first two, adding the fact that our levels of Quality needed improvement as viewed by our Customers. Continuing on, I said that respect was at the foundation of all of my actions.

It became evident to me that all 3 questions were the result of the tone and the culture fostered by management and then engaged by the extended leadership of the UAW. Then I stated that I looked forward to building a team with them, founded in deep respect, and a clear vision to serve our

Customers and our Team Members. The meeting continued for a bit more and then concluded.

I well understood the reason for these 3 questions. They were generated from a management environment that created an atmosphere of tension and hostility in their plants, from years of systemic neglect of the enterprise, and most importantly, from the lack of respect due to them as workers and human beings. They were good people. Trust had been eroded, exposing only pain as a form of expression. They were not used to someone with my beliefs as a GM Executive leader at their location.

Upon immediate reflection, I knew that the atmosphere of Wisconsin-Needmore had been driven to the vilest forms of human interaction that I had ever witnessed in my professional life. I firmly believed, as Deming alludes to, "That ultimately it is management that sets the culture and the tone." Here at Wisconsin-Needmore it had been denigrated to this level.

A foundation of respect had to be established. Plus my self-control would be put to a test with this and the racially motivated insults. I quickly put a rosary ring in my pocket that I carried on this job every day. It was not necessarily to pray with, although that occurred too rarely, but to touch when levels of disrespect were exposed to me. It gave me an immediate tool to touch and "count to 10" in one second before reacting.

> *"You get used to the darkness*
> *You then begin to see in the darkness*
> *You then begin to think that it is light*
> *The abnormal becomes normal"*

(UAW Worker commenting on the reality of Wisconsin-Needmore at an All Employee Communication Meeting on 11/14/96)

We also had a very strange phenomena occurring in the plant that was brought to my attention by a group of African-American workers. They came to visit me in my office late one evening around 8 pm. This occurred after being at Wisconsin-Needmore for 4 months.

They shared a small "hang man's noose" with me. They told me that at times, upon returning to their places of work, they would find these on their workstations. I asked them how long this had been occurring and they told me for years. I asked if they believed that management was aware of this. Their response was "yes." I told them that I would address this immediately.

Since we had established a standardized 16 one-hour meeting cadence for All Employee meetings, I placed a call to Joe and to Mark and explained what happened. I asked that we begin meeting now and extend non-stop, till we ended the cycle, by asking our family to help us stop this most abhorrent and disrespectful act. Joe was most supportive. Together we asked that this cease, as it violated principles in our shared values at Wisconsin-Needmore. It did. We needed to change at Wisconsin-Needmore. We did, not me.

Listening is a skill that is very critical to leaders. Many who move up listen less, when in fact the opposite should happen. Mr. Larry Kessler of GM sat with me when I became a Managing Director for a portion of Mexico. He told me that in this new and larger role it was vital to listen to the staff group that supported me, and furthermore I should find deeper ways to enhance listening to others. I never forgot this lesson. I only wish that I could have practiced it more deeply than I did. Yet at Wisconsin-Needmore, I must now admit that I had great support from someone outside of GM.

I enjoy reading and I read the transcripts of the 13 days of the Cuban Missile Crisis. I then documented how much time President Kennedy actually spoke as opposed to listening. Although not done with mathematical precision, I can say he only spoke about 5% of the time. When he did, he synthesized many great ideas. I think this is an example to all leaders, especially in a time of crisis.

I listened to many people at GM and Wisconsin-Needmore during the post-strike state of healing and resolution. Dialogue leads the way to mutual understanding, but I also realized that as leaders one cannot just seek counsel from within. At Wisconsin-Needmore with its frenetic pace, often times one can get caught up only speaking to other GM'ers. Just as Flint produced a form of inbreeding in terms of thought, so too can an enterprise in crisis just by the nature of the long days and the people you are naturally around.

Although this can be enlightening in context, it is also vital to develop intellectual outlets for discourse in high pressure assignments that are outside of the firm. During my time at Wisconsin-Needmore, a friend from grammar school who was a cabinet member in the Governor's Office of the State of Illinois, helped me navigate many tough issues, challenges, and decisions. A lawyer by training and a natural dynamic leader, Ara was a source of great wisdom that suddenly arrived like a gift from the Almighty! Ara is smart, intelligent, has deep levels of practical common sense, and has the ability to navigate political minefields. In short, the perfect complementary voice of reason to a job called by GM is toughest. I am deeply indebted to Ara, for her insights and support to me about the deep enterprise issues. Her counsel as to the timing of strategic actions and the final contractual language of the agreement were outstanding. Her ability to help so many people unselfishly is a true form of servant leadership through caring and counsel. On behalf of the many at Wisconsin-Needmore I would like to now thank her! We should have paid her. But knowing Ara and her humility, she would have gladly turned down compensation. It was done pro-bono. Just another example of a great Human Being!

I was asked to lead at Wisconsin-Needmore. In so doing, I had to set a very pronounced example of respect with great and wonderful people. These people deserved this and more importantly hungered for it as human beings. It had been denied to them for a very long time.

We (Union and Management) attempted to do this by building a system and exposing our culture at Wisconsin-Needmore. We did this by exposing our own inherent light, not the darkness of shadows that had become prevalent and normal in a most unnatural way there.

We did this with:

- The Commitment to share Leadership with Respect in all our enterprise actions.

174

- The establishment of Guiding Values that were fully defined.
    - People
    - Safety/Environment
    - Customers
    - Teamwork
    - Continuous Improvement
    - Winning
    - Communication
    - Organizational Structure

- Policies/Procedures: The development of a business plan with the Union with metrics.
- The development of a safety plan with the Union with metrics.
- Joint meetings with the Union and all members on a monthly basis to review metrics and performance during 12-16 consecutive 1 hour meetings.
- Open questions at all meetings with employees; any question was taken - no filters.
- The development of an "Employee Knowledge Clock" with our collective years of knowledge on it that was constantly being updated like the population clock. We had roughly 90,000 years of collective experience accumulating 12.2 years a day. We either respected it or engaged it or it was wasted through the disrespect of non-engagement. We tried to do the former.

- We established memorials at both major complexes to honor both past and present Wisconsin-Needmore Team Members in a visual mural-like way.
- We established a Memorial to all UAW workers who lost their lives while working.
- We aligned all our plans to GM-Delphi.
- We established 7 plant Communication Stations to share all vital plant metrics in a standardized way.
- We developed a guide book with definitions and examples on how to interpret all plant performance charts.
- We built a foundation of business and safety, then planning a deployment. We then set our sights on human development. This was done by creating the winner's profile of attributes required to "win" for our Customer, with specific examples from our plants.
- We built a "Learning Pyramid" with attributes for individual learning and performance that aligned with our enterprise objectives.
- We created an award called the "Water Carrier" that was given to team members who exemplified its definition through their actions in support of our :
  – Business Plan
  – Safety Plan
  – Winners Profile
  – Learning Pyramid

- We established, shared and aligned all 7 plants with Key Metrics in the objectives of Safety-Quality-Cost-Fast-Great-Customer Focus.

- We established a standard problem solving process with the visual aid of a football field.

- We established the only permitted form of graffiti in our plant through the Continuous Improvement Wall. This is where we tracked all of our improvements along the lines of our objectives.

- We established free blood pressure machines in our plants to enhance awareness around personal health and safety.

- We established a fast protocol for responses to Customer concerns globally in less than one hour. We gave all our Customers a 24 hour card with names and numbers to call in case of an issue.

- We established value definition note cards that were used in meetings to take notes that served to reinforce our shared values.

- We established a supervisor clipboard with standardized actions, in each of our objective areas, with a pronounced focus on safety actions in case of an accident or chemical spill.

- We established an enterprise wide daily communication system, on all safety and quality issues, that was shared daily results.

- We established a supervisor handbook, with the details of our operating system, which were shared with all team members.
- We established a balanced scorecard that led to strategic planning.
- We gave all team members an operating focus book that shared the essence of the Wisconsin-Needmore System that we had put into place.
- Our tours were conducted primarily by our UAW Brothers and Sisters with support from management.
- We negotiated the first GM-UAW 6 Year Agreement with a 10 Year no strike clause in USA history.

**"The Water Carrier" Award at Wisconsin-Needmore**

*An essential part of all societies from the early city states to modern civilizations today is the availability and accessibility of water. In many societies the water carrier was a vital part of their rituals as well as nourishment and thus life! This same duality of the spiritual and practical uses of water are evident in our society today. In short, water is life, and therefore the carrier of water is the bringer of life.*

*A manufacturing plant is a microcosm of society, and as such we have our Wisconsin-Needmore set of rituals and nourishment that sustains our organizational life. Many people comprise our Business, each intrinsically valuable to the overall well-being and evolution of our business.*

178

*Yet, there are those individuals who truly bring life to our organization by demonstrating a spirit of humanity, ingenuity, tireless efforts and dedication to the survival of our business. These very people are our water carriers. Their actions bring life and hence provide us with the opportunity to see tomorrow.*

All we really did together at Wisconsin-Needmore was to naturally share leadership with wonderful, great, and talented people. We began to see the sun together, come in from the shadows, and work with clarity and respect, just as the UAW worker stated early in the post-strike timeframe there. (11/14/96)

GM C-Suite leadership was very concerned with Wisconsin-Needmore since the initial massive strike in July of 1996. In my previous roles at GM I had on occasion hosted major leadership visits to the sites under my responsibility. However, they were very few and far between. This changed when I was at Wisconsin-Needmore. Because of the strike prior to my arrival, we were on the major radar screen of the company. We had more visits in the 32 months I spent there than I had in all my prior assignments combined.

The worry at Wisconsin-Needmore was real and GM wanted to begin to see progress. Mr. Jack Smith was the CEO of GM at the time and he visited us on more than one occasion. He was a quiet and pensive man who I respected a great deal. His leadership was felt and respected in a direct yet very humble way. On plant tours he would often stray from the tour route to go meet people and greet them.

179

He was a sinccrc person and that sincerity was translated to those around him.

On his first visit to our plants he entered our Needmore facility and was greeted by line workers. This, in an environment that only a few months earlier, had seen workers walking a picket line. I could sense that both Mr. Smith and the group of C suite executives were somewhat taken aback. After reviewing the Worker Memorial Mural that we had built at the entrances to both of our facilities, which was made with photos of workers both past and present, no one could fail to see a huge digital device that hung above the entrance to the main plant. We had installed it months earlier as the momentum for our efforts of change at Wisconsin-Needmore began to take hold.

Part of this system, was a digital counter, akin to the ones that depict the population of the Earth, constantly adding people. At Wisconsin-Needmore we put a spin on the digital counter and with the aid of 2 brilliant engineers who calculated the algorithm, we were able to depict what we called the Employee Knowledge Clock. The clock ran out to about 6 decimal places so it could be constantly moving and adding.

Collectively, we had over 90,000 years of knowledge among the seniority levels of our 4500 + employees accumulating 12.2 years of additional knowledge every working day at Wisconsin-Needmore! When Mr. Smith walked by he saw the device and asked about its meaning. I told him its essence, the power of collective knowledge, our movement to be one team where the impossible could be possible, and the reality that the greatest form of disrespect is to not engage our team members in our business.

Ninety thousand years of knowledge is an awfully powerful source by which to catalyze positive change. Our objective at Wisconsin-Needmore was to build a system around people and to build a culture of improvement upon our legacy. I can only say that the expression on his face said to me that we at Wisconsin-Needmore had given him a gift of a new way of looking at our most valuable resource, people! He was positively stricken! This was, in essence, what we tried to build at Wisconsin-Needmore. Mr. Smith and other leaders expressed their gratitude.

We recognized many water carriers at Wisconsin-Needmore, great people, and great acts of difference! The water and people have always been a part of GM; sometimes we only just occasionally provided the tools rather than creating a "system" of perpetual buckets! Great People!

Right after Wisconsin-Needmore, I became the Global Quality Director for Alan Dawes, at the Automotive Components Chassis Group (ACG). I think that one of the big things that we did there, was to develop a system, to react to Customers and Customer concerns. We reinforced our systems and philosophy of Quality and Customer focus. We started this at Wisconsin-Needmore, where we would assess where we were with our Customers on a daily basis.

This enables us to be categorized in both areas of Quality and Delivery. The attention that we paid to Quality really improved our position with our Customers, as it would reflect on the areas, where we needed to go to work, to make improvements. Since we had been doing this process while at Wisconsin-Needmore, I think this was part of the reason they decided to send me to my next assignment at the ACG level.

We had a system of Customer Support Engineers that we specifically assigned to plants. In my new role, I would receive reports back each day from a global perspective. In this way we could specifically determine where we needed help to address issues. And every day, I would send out a voice-message globally, to all the Leaders of the ACG, as well as all the plant managers. The message would include all the defects that we had and more importantly, what we were doing about it.

Now this process upset a lot of plant managers. The reason was because it tended to be embarrassing. But bringing plant problems to the forefront enabled us to determine where to go to work. Red is good! Let's now do something about this! A global message being sent out that identified a Quality issue, in one specific plant location, enabled us to react faster using limited resources. One plant manager thought that I was "airing out his dirty laundry." I tried to explain to him that awareness was a good thing and support to that end was vital on our part. Turning red to green was all of our jobs and then making it even a deeper shade of green!

Just like in medicine, you have to be made aware of the root cause before you can determine what the fix can be. A year later, when the GM bonus time came around, I literally saw and heard from people who were so grateful for having their issues addressed and making Customers happy. The Quality improvement and reduction in Quality issues/defects had a direct correlation on profitability. The executive bonuses go up, as the overall Quality improves. That is not really the reason that I implemented this process. The fact of the matter is that I think the biggest thing we accomplished, is that we could do this. We did it even though we did not have the shared deep culture of a Toyota-like system.

My next assignment was that of Business Line Executive for Delphi. After this, I went back to GM as a Director of Program Management for small cars in North America. My next stop was at GM Powertrain and Assembly in Mexico. That is where I ended my career with GM in 2007, upon the untimely death of my father. My most powerful learning took place at Wisconsin-Needmore and at Toyota.

At this point in time, I wanted to make a career change. In 2007 when I left GM, I entered the University of Texas El Paso (UTEP) as an adjunct professor. At that time, I also entered UTEP as the Director of Latin American Studies. Additionally, at that time, I was an adjunct professor in the School of Business. During my time at UTEP, I have to give credit to all the people who have made me who I am. From my parents to Dr. Fuller, GM, the Jesuits, Toyota and beyond, they have all been a part of my success. I have been blessed with 6 academic awards for teaching, 3 departmental awards, and then 3 as the top teacher in the Business Graduate School. The learning, experiences, and lessons of my life given to me through so many wonderful people did this. Not me, I simply just transmitted their spirit to our students. These acknowledgements were determined by our Customers, the students!

In 2012 in the State of Texas, I was also blessed to be rated as one of the 14 best Hispanic Professors in the state. The reason for this is because people recognized that the instruction, or my process of teaching, was that I tried to impart to each student all the learnings that I had accumulated in a unique Socratic format. This is coming from the 90% of the rank/file and the 10% of the executives. I made an effort to bring these teachings into the classroom. Just like the clock at Wisconsin-Needmore accumulated knowledge and its power and wisdom so did I, as gifts from the people who touched me my whole life. I simply gave to others what others gave to me.

I get my energy to do what I do from our students, as they are super! Thank you! I am most grateful to the UT administration and Dr. Diana Natalicio that allows me this opportunity at this point in my life.

One other thing that I do with all my courses is to "Benchmark" them with others. This is a common practice in the auto industry that can be readily applied to any field. I benchmarked my courses with graduate courses at the some of our leading business schools in the USA and beyond. I wanted to ensure that what I gave my students would be equal to or better than what was being taught at those other institutions.

Given the fact that we were not normally highly rated as a university from an MBA perspective, I have created all of my courses very academically and intellectually challenging for the students. Using the Socratic Participant-Centered method of learning, I choose practical books and models used in executive education at a corporate level, coupled with real Harvard Business School cases. This builds the body of our course. This in turn is complemented and enhanced with the great experiences that I had at GM and Toyota. I have very high expectations from my students in the graduate classes, just like I had at our Wisconsin-Needmore Team.

After some time at UTEP I made the decision to go back into the car business with Toyota. I was offered a position in Europe as the COO in that location. I determined that this offer was an outstanding way to go back to manufacturing. The Toyota assignment would be very challenging and be an offer of a lifetime. The headquarters for this assignment were in both Brussels and Munich. We were building new businesses.

I had a unique experience while in Europe. I was offered the Presidency of Toyota Boshoku Europe by Dr. Toyoda. That was going to be announced in April of 2014. What came into play though was my mom's health. With the need to be close to her, I really could not accept that position. Number one, my mom did not want to come to Germany. And, as a result of her not wanting to come, and a 5 year commitment to that position in Europe, I respectfully declined to our senior Leadership.

Although it was an incredible honor for the offer, and even to be considered, I considered it best for me and my family not to take the position. My time as COO, under the leadership of Dr. Toyoda was the most balanced and complete assignment in my life. Toyota is a strong unselfish culture of respect and support for the worker. Their philosophy of support for the worker was shared by me prior to my role as COO and my time there only reinforced this.

Toyota and the Toyoda Family are the most honorable people I have ever worked with. I am blessed for their support of me and the learning that was freely given to me. Dr. Toyoda and my sensei Kidokoro-san are solid pillars from whom I still reflect upon for guidance to this day.

Based upon my decision at Toyota, I made a decision to return to UTEP. After returning to UTEP, I continued my concept of a "support session" for students. These sessions are in effect tutoring sessions. What I do is dedicate a Friday afternoon or Saturday to these sessions.

I tell students that I am going to be in this room to discuss anything that they want. I will be there for 8 hours on Saturday, to provide them with any support in writing a brief, how to write a paper, how to write a case, how to analyze a case, how to analyze a financial statement, or balance sheet. Whatever their needs, I will be there to help them. If I do not now know, I will find out.

You can walk into the room that I am in at any time for help. Inevitably, I will sit in the room and students will begin to walk in intermittently. Sometimes they come in as a single person, sometimes as a number together to discuss similar or different subject matter. They can be both graduate and undergraduate students. Normally I teach graduate students, but I never hesitate to help undergraduate students. I think that is a very good thing, because students initially come in for help in a certain class, but then the discussion evolves into their career. The act of mentoring is a natural by-product of these sessions for these students.

It is an investment of my time. But I really think that it is important to be able to close this incredible gap, which many of our students possess in their academic life. I have a classic example. I once met a person many years ago with a 4 year degree in French, yet she could not speak French.

Now, I use this analogy or metaphor to make the case for what I see in business schools. I want to do my part to ensure the "basic fluency" of our students in business. What I have done for the business students is to share a set of models that will help or assist the students, which I used as a board member and COO.

Since my career had spanned GM and Toyota, I created these symbols or hieroglyphics, which allow me to interpret various business situations. So if you will, I have hieroglyphics memorized in my mind, which are symbols or charts, with words and clues. Quite honestly, when I sat on the board in Europe, I used them frequently.

If you think about it, it can be very intimidating to go into a room with a number of people to discuss major issues. This, along with the complexity of business issues, or current financial problems, can make for an uneasy experience. But, through the use of my models, I was able to distinguish problem areas as well as solutions. These are the same hieroglyphics that I attempt to instill in my students. I do this, so that they can be fluent in the language of business, so that when they leave the university, they are capable of speaking business. This applies to both graduate and undergraduate students. So I made a promise to myself, to dedicate an awful lot of time to these students, with these support sessions. At times these sessions turned into their personal mentoring sessions. I will go and assist when and where I can.

An example is that a short time ago I spoke at an APICS Student Conference. All I showed them were slides of Japan, intermixed with slides from a Toyota assembly plant. While showing these slides, I played Japanese music. But, during that PowerPoint presentation, I described the nature of TPS. I didn't really discuss any specific tools, but just the nature, philosophy, and the cultural aspect. The long and short of it, is that even though I am taking a lot of my time to help others, it is a great benefit for them. That is what makes it worthwhile.

In another example, I was going to be teaching a financial support class to 40 students, where all of them have stated that they were weak in finance. So, I have a module from Harvard, that even I can understand, and they will understand as well. We walked through it and talked about it so that they had an understanding of what it all means. Hopefully, they will walk away from this session with something in their back pocket, which will be useful to them in the future. So that 10 years from now, if they have a problem with cash flow, they will be able to reach back, and use what was discussed to resolve their issue.

They can use this class as well as the hieroglyphics that I used in the past myself, as a tool to solve their problems. One other thing that I think is important is that because of all the great people that I worked with at GM, even the ones that disagreed with me, I learned from them as well. The typical graduate school professor teaches at most, 3 or 4 different courses. What I have been able to do is teach 12 different graduate classes thanks to GM and Toyota.

The answer to the reason that I can do it is because I worked at GM and Toyota. I worked with great people at GM and Toyota that taught me a lot. I teach 12 different classes at the graduate level, which is a pretty heavy and diverse load. But, GM was a diverse organization, which really helped me to help others. It is just like I was tutoring kids back at Midtown. I really enjoyed that, just as I am enjoying it today. I have found that you learn the most in the toughest assignments.

When I think back while in high school, I was doing very, very badly in Latin. But, one of the best top 3 or 4 teachers that I ever had was a gentleman by the name of Frank Raispis at St. Ignatius. He was a Latin teacher who, after school on his own time, had a classroom that was opened up to anyone that was having a problem with Latin. Anyone was welcomed in that classroom for help. I remember I was there every day because I was not very good initially as a Latin student. But the Mr. Raispis "technique" of what he did to help me move to the A zone as well as so many others, is what I am doing today.

If I look back on my life and career, I think that to a large extent I have tried to do what is right in a deep and special way, applied to situations of management. These vary in degrees of complexity and impact to people and to businesses. It is in those critical moments that one defines oneself. I have made many mistakes, but keep learning. I have also tried to help others and in so, doing link that effort to the sustainability of the enterprise.

A dear friend comes to mind at this crucial stage in my thoughts. His name is Ron James. He was the director of finance at Wisconsin-Needmore when I arrived there, but beyond that title he is a brilliant and exceptional human being. Let me now tell you why. Ron was not a GM man. He was a man who answered and guided himself by far higher standards. His acumen at finance and accounting was unmatched by any other person I have interacted with professionally. He also was a wonderful member of our team at Wisconsin-Needmore because he could really help us release tension with very insightful and light hearted anecdotes. After I left Wisconsin-Needmore, I went on several international assignments and one of the most painful parts of that event are taxes. Although the company would pay very well-known accounting firms to do our taxes, I always felt that their work was more of an act of presence in helping executives as, opposed to truly making a difference for us. So during one of these filing periods I happened to call Ron about another matter, and as always, he asked how things were going. I told him that I was in the middle of taxes and he said to send him all the paperwork. This was not the intention of our conversation, but Ron is Ron. He wanted to help. Well, not only did Ron find things these New York accounting firms did not find, he corrected them and taught them a thing or two.

190

I decided to pay Ron, even though he refused to accept any money. I sent him a check. Years later we were speaking and he told me a story of his daughter and a lesson that he taught her about friendship. He told her that he pointed to the wall where a check was framed like a piece of art. It was the check that I sent to Ron years before. He never cashed it. He told his daughter why. That being my friend, he helped me. The daughter quickly asked him if she could take the check and cash it. He reiterated the story again and the meaning of friendship to her. Ron's friendship lesson for me has never been lost nor has his spirit. It still guides me to this day. One final note, as you have surmised, I am not good at balancing my checkbook. But I am blessed with a great friend!

The path that one takes in life is often dictated very early on and based on your decisions. Therefore, I believe the key question is, why I made the decisions I made, expressing my leadership process with others, in the fashion that I did.

My childhood established some very key values in me. They gave me a sense of "true north." Experiences and guidance in school, as well as the workplace, allowed me to ensure and calibrate the accuracy of my compass over time. Yet to this day, it is still the compass my parents gave to me. I continue to learn. I continue to calibrate.

One can say that I was a first generation person growing up in the states. My dad was from Mexico and my ma from the border with Mexico and the USA, essentially a marginalized place from the USA. In many ways as such, I consider myself a 1 to 1.5 generation person in this country. I think this is more vital to me now than it was when I was younger. Assimilation into the context of the culture in the USA, is unique when balancing the components of your past (ancestors), with the ground that you walk today. In my case, I have walked an awful lot in the USA, but my steps represent each culture (USA/Mexican) with every pace. My direction, no matter where I am at on the planet, reflects this while I continue to learn. Learning in a global context is very important for me.

The Greeks said that happiness "is the pursuit of your abilities along lines of excellence." I really "dig" this. We all have very distinct abilities and I truly believe that is what makes our world so great.

As a child, I was taught to respect others. My dad would quote Juarez of Mexico all the time to me: "Respect for the rights of others is peace." My mother was very strict and despite never having the opportunity to go to college, both my parents instilled learning in me.

If I did not have enough homework my Ma always gave me more! They would buy used teachers' books. They said my interest grew in certain areas. They would sacrifice themselves and buy me books on evolution, archaeology and anthropology. I am looking at some as I write today. I will never let them go in a spiritual sense.

Chicago is a rich place for poor people! In spite of our economic condition, my parents would regularly take my two sisters and me to museums. Quickly, I was drawn to natural history, archaeology, anthropology and art. We would go to the Oriental Institute of the University of Chicago, where the study of the archaeology of the Middle East was its

192

theme. I learned to love Egypt and mummies. When visiting my relatives in Mexico, we often took trips to nearby archaeological sites where my deep fascination with ancient history and my place in it had deep meaning to me.

I grew up in a tough neighborhood in Chicago, a very tough place on 18th street. It was and still is a Mexican neighborhood with people like myself, not many second generation types. Unfortunately, many Mexican gangs existed there. Going to school in the morning was a gauntlet of sorts. I learned to look at my surroundings with every step and to find alternate ways of getting to my destination. I learned all the back alleys very well. As I got older, defending me diminished a great deal, since the people who chased me, understood that my interests were in school, sports and other items. I also learned that in order to move forward, sometimes you have to quickly take a step back or find an alternate way.

In that sense, I can say that the gangs were very respectful after a time. They respected my choice and looked to others for support. Where I lived was a very cool place to be loved and to learn in, in spite of the violence of young people. I knew this very well as it was around me. Young people were dying.

The Vietnam War was going on and my parents were both very much against it. They would encourage us to speak about politics around the table. I had a jean jacket with a peace patch sewn on it by my ma. I thought it was very cool. I still have the patch today on a bigger jean jacket!

As mentioned earlier, my earliest conscious memory was watching my parents cry in front of our TV set on the day that President Kennedy died. I was frightened as I did not understand what was going on at that time. Today, I can reflect on that moment in time in terms of change. Leaders have a deep responsibility to people; at times I feel at the expense of their own lives. If a business is troubled, often times only leaders know the true essence of its decay while attempting to navigate solutions while never passing on to others a sense of despair or hopelessness. To those whom much is given, much is expected. It comes while helping to insulate others of the pain, if it were to come until the very end, yet bearing the pain.

Yet change is the catalyst for action. I often remember a prayer or anecdote that was once shared with me by a Jesuit. "When I was young, I asked God for the ability to help change the world and make it a better place for all. But by the time I was middle aged, realizing that I did not accomplish much, I then began to ask God for the ability to help change those around me. Now that I am an old man I realize that I should have asked God from the very beginning to help change me. For if I had asked this from the very beginning I would not have wasted my life."

Waste in a Toyota sense, is the most egregious manifestation of management, and its structures in the workplace. All efforts should be directed to its elimination. Yet the precursor to the elimination of waste is the ability to change. Yet the ability to change is tenuous in most organizations. Some are systemically more adept than others. Some

194

are more philosophically and culturally established to drive change than others.

I remember that I once read a definition of "primitive" by the famous Anthropologist Levi-Strauss. He stated that primitive equates to the desire of a group, who do not want to change, preferring to remain in the condition that the gods created them in. I was always fascinated by this idea.

Today, I tell my students that I have met many primitive people in my life, but not in the places that you might imagine. I did not encounter primitive thoughts or actions in the Mato Grosso of Brasil nor in the highlands of Papua New Guinea among the Answats. Often times I have encountered the primitive in the corridors of power of corporations, places that at times, were the antithesis of courageous change. Where power and their classes preferred to remain in the same state where they were created in by their gods in the enterprise. This idea seems to apply to many places on our planet besides corporations.

With time, with my parents, grandparents, a Jesuit education, and the great people I have been blessed to work with in GM, Toyota and the University of Texas, I have been on a trek to assimilate the many dimensions of what leadership should be. I learned how people can express it. I also learned how leaders are expected to express it, in the face of the temptation to do otherwise. In my last corporate assignment at Toyota, the lady who helped me administratively asked how I wanted the name plate outside my door to read. I asked that the COO be removed and replaced with "Trying to be Human" with my name after this.

"How Do I Measure My Life" is a work by a Dr. Clayton Christensen from the Harvard Business School. In his article he speaks to many dimensions of our work lives and its necessity for reflection, yet to me what is vital from his piece is that leaders need to make space and time to reflect about their plan and their life.

My personal Dr. Christenson is Jim Villella, the author of this book, and Ron James. I was blessed to meet Jim and Ron many years ago. In fact, I would dare say even before we were reacquainted at Wisconsin-Needmore I seemed to know them. Jim has catalyzed all of these thoughts for me. For that I shall be eternally grateful!

In summary, I have determined it is not what you do or the position you hold in life that sets you apart, it is the "How" you do it. How you lead and, most importantly, how you treat others. I firmly believe that the greatest leaders in the world are not only the ones you read about or see in business journals. But the many who live in the silence of their humble yet profound examples and gifts to others. They made me, and in large part they made us!

While living, I just keep trying to learn, knowing that I still have a long, long, way to go as a leader, and more importantly as a human being. In the final analysis, that is all that I am.

**Robin & Charles Hawkins**
**Business Field:** Dental Practice
**Business Name:** Charles Hawkins, Jr., D.D.S., Inc.
**Current Positions:** Secretary/President

## Personal Backgrounds:
### Charles Hawkins:

My father was a dentist and later became the first black man to graduate from Ohio State's Orthodontic program. He then became an Orthodontist practicing in Middletown, Ohio. I always wanted to follow in my father's footsteps. Unfortunately, he passed away at the age of 45 to Lou Gehrig's disease when I was 19 years old. I then became the head of the household and was expected to take care of things as my dad had done.

After my undergraduate studies were completed at Ohio University, I came home to help my mother and worked for 5 years at the Simpson Paper Mill, before making the decision that it was time to go back to school to complete my dental degree. I found that this part of my life was a very trying time. I knew that if I made it through dental school, I would do everything I could to help people and make my practice successful.

### Robin Williams-Hawkins:

I knew at a young age that I wanted to be a dental hygienist and went to college for several years for that specific purpose. While Chuck was in dental school, I was an orthodontic assistant and loved it. I planned on completing my degree as a hygienist after he was done with his schooling. However, things went in a different direction for me and I ended up

197

on the financial end of our practice. I enjoyed the challenges of learning the financial aspect of running a business and that has been my position ever since. I think the accounting position is a much better fit for me. I find it amazing that we were both interested in dentistry before having met each other and then working together to complete our dream, of him becoming a dentist, and us having our own dental practice.

Our mindset is of having everyone trained to do what needs to be done. All of our staff represents our business. This includes, but not limited to, ensuring that everyone is thoroughly trained on any new or current equipment. We also ensure that everyone that works at the office learns about successful management techniques, running an organization, etc.

We really try to treat everyone, the people that work for us, as well as our patients, like family. Chuck and I both listen to our patients, regarding their concerns as well as their ideas. We let the staff know that they are sincerely appreciated, as we can't do everything ourselves, nor should we try.

We have both taken a lot of continuing education courses, as well as staying up with current technology, which has been part of our success. As an example, we use IV sedation for patients that are hesitant for a certain procedure, whether young or old.

We have also utilized same day crowns and bridges for many people that cannot take off time from their families or their jobs. We try to save them their time and effort, which equates to dollars and cents to them, because their time is valuable. Since we do not want to have a large number of patients waiting, we try to schedule to keep the chairs filled. No one wants to wait, especially if they are in pain.

A common theory was that Orthodontics was a special service for many of our kids. This may have been true in the past for "vanity" purposes as a teen, but now many older folks are coming in because they can finally afford it. We use a concept of "invisible trays" so the straightening process is not as noticeable

We also found that many of our patients have or had suffered from sleep apnea. We do not use a Continuous Positive Airway Pressure (CPAP). We use an oral device appliance which is a lot less restrictive than a traditional mask. It is an excellent alternative for those that can't wear the CPAP.

For our "major dental procedures" we provide our cell phone number, as well as our home number, to patients that may be apprehensive after a major dental process.

To ensure that everything works from a theory of being financially acceptable, we put everything down on paper. We have to see the benefits for us and our patients, as well as shortcomings to an idea or concept, so that we have a good chance of success before going forward.

As a staff, we also review what we need to be doing this week as well as next week in our office to ensure that we have a "game plan' for the coming days, weeks, and months. To accomplish this, we have mid-day staff meetings when the patient load is minimal. We have found out with our historical data that early mornings and late afternoons are our peak periods for our patients. Since we want our staff meetings to be productive, the mid-day sessions have worked out well.

Any major equipment purchases are thoroughly reviewed before a final decision is made. One of the first questions that we ask ourselves is, will it be a benefit to our patients, and then will it be beneficial for our practice? Of course we have an accountant that advises us in the areas of our process of evaluating new equipment. This consists of a financial evaluation such as return on investment, payback, and depreciation. But we also take into consideration the benefit to the patient. Recently we purchased an oral scanning device for cancer screening. It is a light that shines in the mouth to detect any oral cancer. If we have an area of concern, we send a sample to the lab to determine if it is cancerous or not.

We found out early in our business career, that dental school did not teach you anything about trying to open a practice, maintain that practice, or grow that practice.

We do not out-source anything as we are personally responsible for payroll, taxes, insurance, and 401K plans for ourselves and office staff. We personally review all incoming invoices for the practice. We do have quarterly meetings with our accountant, to ensure that we are on track with our projections.

Initially, we started out with 1 room and 1 chair in a rented facility in 1997. Then we went to a 4 chair practice, finally evolving into an 8 chair practice today.

We quickly outgrew our facility and needed to expand. We had to make a business decision early on to either continue leasing or purchase the entire building we were in.

One of the most important and intelligent decisions that we ever made was to buy the building so that we may expand. This also provided us the control of the other tenants around us. As you know, if you don't own, you can't control the tenants around you. As we all know the owner may make decisions beneficial to her/him. This may or may not be in the best interest of your business.

In the beginning, we worked full-time days, evenings, and weekends. But when your personal family starts growing, there has to be time for them. This time with them is used to provide your philosophy to them. As such, we had to bring on additional staff as our personal family began to grow. Continued training of all our staff was critical when we started our practice and has been ever since.

One of our hygienists became our marketing "officer." She went out publicly to establish our advertising process, creating billboards, and worked with radio and TV stations for our commercials. Since our business is very competitive, you have to set yourself apart from others. Now, through that process, she has grown to own her own business, and still makes referrals back to us.

We now have 1 full time person devoted to marketing our office. She works with our radio and television people as well as many other marketing strategies.

We have weekly staff meetings to brainstorm new ideas and concepts that may or may not contribute to the success of our business. This includes *all* staff personnel. We found an interesting concept. If your staff has the proper information and understanding of where the dental practice is going, they can provide implementation and action items for your success. Remember, they are an integral part of *the* business, not *our* business.

We do a lot of advertising, but our success has come from word-of-mouth. We have radio and TV commercials. Speaking of word-of-mouth, one of the ideas that came out of our staff meetings was to send some type of gift to a student who has had their braces removed. We send the gift, such as balloons and candy, (none that would cause tooth decay and provide additional business for us) to celebrate the occasion. Since kids are sometimes self-conscious of having braces in the first place, they really enjoy some type of celebration in front of their peers, when their braces are removed.

We also email and text smile reminders on a frequent basis, just to remind everyone of our services, and checkups.

We also remind everyone that has dental insurance, that if you have money left over at the end of the year, there may be some extra benefit that we provide, where you can use your benefit instead of losing it.

An interesting concept that we discovered is, if we are "out of network," with some of our patient's insurance, we may lose them because they may not want to pay more out of pocket expenses. And it may be less expensive for them to go to a dentist that takes their insurance. However, many find out that the quality of care is not the same as it is in our office and they often return to us. The criteria for making a decision may not always be a financial one. Based on a lot of our historical data regarding customers, a lot of our previous customers have come back to us, even though we are out of their network. When we talk to them about why they left and later returned, most always the answer is service!

Orthodontics has been a huge part of our business. People may not always spend money on themselves, but will make sure their children's teeth are straight. Technology has changed greatly over the years. We use a Cerec machine that makes same day crowns, bridges, digital x-rays, and cancer screening devices. Digital cameras enable the patient to actually see the deterioration of the teeth for themselves. You have to stay up with technology. But remember, that we apply the technology and it is not something that you can buy off the shelf and use instantly. Training for the proper use of technology is always critical.

During our staff meetings, we always use an agenda for items for discussion and follow-up. Our office manager runs the meetings using this agenda. After the agenda items are completed, we come up with a "To Do List" which consists of the item to be addressed, who is responsible for addressing the item, and a due date for item completion. This allows all of us to know what is transpiring in "our" business for the future. Everyone is kept in the "loop" with our minutes from our meetings.

One of the other major components of maintaining our success is cross-training. As we have a large number of female staff, there is a need for time off, as well as extended time off. Since we all have this philosophy in our mind at our practice, we can continue the business on a day to day basis, with transparency to our customers.

Based on our success, we do a free dental day, usually once a year, to give back to the community. We try to help the people that don't have dental insurance or that may put off dental treatment due to cost. All of our staff donate their time as well. It has been a blessing to our patients who take advantage of this service, ourselves, and the office staff as well.

We will provide a variety of services whether it's a cleaning, filling, extraction, or whatever is most pressing for them. We also donate toothbrushes and toothpaste for various organizations.

We also randomly help patients and their relatives if they are having a personal tough time. For example; a grandmother had received custody of a grandchild and the child needed dental work. The grandmother does not have insurance so the grandmother couldn't afford it. We did it for free. There have been many cases similar to this over the years. We really believe that, if you do good for others, it comes back to you. We like to think of it as "Putting Good Karma" out there.

**Roy Link**
**Business Field:** Engineering - Design and Manufacture of Test Equipment and Provider of Testing Services
**Business Name:** Link Engineering Company/Link Testing Services
**Current Position:** Chairman & CEO, Link Engineering Company

**Personal Background:**

I was born in Detroit, Michigan on October 24, 1944, and was raised on the west side of the city. My parents were Martha and Herbert Link. Both were born and grew up in Besigheim, Germany. They were next door neighbors during their youth. As economic conditions were not good in Germany in the 1920s, they both came to the US with plans to stay for two years, to earn money to support their families. In the end, they never returned to Germany permanently, but rather married and grew their family in the US.

I have 3 sisters, all older than I. Margaret passed away in her early 50s, Anita is 82, living in Atherton, California. Sigrid is 77, living in Princeton, New Jersey. I have 10 nieces and nephews who are scattered throughout the US.

I was married to Dawn Airey for 30 years. She passed away from colon cancer in 2007. We had three children, Carrie 43, Matthew 41, and Adam 31. I re-married in 2012 to Pegeen Boland. She has two daughters, Pam 28 and Maddie 24, and one son Wes who is 20.

My education included attending Mackenzie High School, graduating in 1962. I graduated from

Michigan State University with a BS Degree in Mechanical Engineering in 1967. Then I went on at MSU and received an MBA in Personnel Business, in 1968.

I worked afternoons and summers at Link Engineering Company during high school and college. These work sessions included a variety of jobs such as mechanical design and work in the shop. At that point in time, I was not really building a career, but just learning some fundamentals of a positive work ethic. I was in the shop on Saturdays and Sundays with my dad, and it was certainly the natural place to go. From the beginning, I really knew that I was destined to end up in my dad's business. Actually, the jobs that I had helped me to learn a diverse number of skill sets, that I would use later on, and which became very beneficial to me. The time spent in the shop provided a hands-on proficiency which would not have been learned after leaving school.

My experience included operating various machines, filing, sanding, buffing, running the blueprint machine, reading drawings, and many others. These all related to disciplines such as quality, workmanship, timeliness, and responsibility. I learned the concept of a machine being designed to perform a specific function and then being detailed and built, part by part.

At Link we start from an existing machine design or from a clean piece of paper, to develop a new machine which must be fabricated, machined, assembled, and checked out before it is delivered to a customer. In the end, we are responsible for making it perform the task the customer expects.

My first official employment was with Burroughs Corporation from 1968 until 1971, as a Senior Systems Analyst. In this position I worked on the implementation of computerized management operating systems, in Burroughs facilities around the world.

My work at Burroughs was part of a 100 man management systems group, which was involved in all management and operational functions, which were in use to manage Burroughs Corporation. At the time, these tasks were typically performed manually. We were charged with the task of converting these operations to computer based functions which could be executed automatically.

In the beginning, I worked on existing programs to make modifications and enhancements as they were needed. This evolved into developing new programs to perform new functions, which allowed for the automation of other business operations within Burroughs. Ultimately, I led a team to define and implement complete operating systems.

For example, the payroll and labor distribution function for a 5,000 person plant in Plymouth was being performed manually, by over 30 clerical workers. A fellow coworker and I analyzed how these functions were being performed. Each task had a time standard which employees worked to. Their pay was based upon how they performed in relation to this work standard. We then developed computer programs to compute payrolls and distribute labor across the appropriate accounts, to enable accurate payouts to employees and allow part costs to be calculated. In addition, I traveled to Burroughs sites around the world, to implement computerized operating systems, which would assist in the management and operation of Burroughs facilities.

I was allowed to emerge from a single contributor to a team leader and project manager. This advancement in responsibilities enabled me to develop management skills, which would serve me well in my future positions at Link. This exposure to the computer and programming protocols also enabled me to understand how the computer functioned. Then I could find out how it could be applied to an entire realm of tasks, thereby exposing me to the benefits of computerization. It also rewarded me with gratification from successfully implementing numerous operating systems. These systems would alter the technique Burroughs would use to manage their entire organization.

My next assignment was moving to Link Engineering as a sales engineer in 1971. This company founded by my father in 1935, when he started making tap wrenches in his basement.

Link Engineering is a designer and manufacturer of special test systems. I progressed through numerous positions within the organization assuming the Presidency in 1982. Link Engineering has grown from 100 employees located in the US, to our current team of nearly 500 employees throughout the world. A key development was the establishment of a testing organization to serve our customers, as Link Testing Laboratories was founded in 1978. Link is recognized as a critical provider of test equipment and testing services by OEM and Tier suppliers in the transportation industry worldwide.

I feel my success started with my upbringing where my parents worked very hard and lived very honestly and frugally. The model they established left a strong influence upon my character. This led to my inherent method for dealing with people I have encountered and worked with, throughout my life.

From that beginning, I have engaged with many outstanding people in school, in business, and in my social life. These people have been a terrific inspiration to me and have allowed me to glean many positive traits which have allowed me to further develop my character and expand my horizons. Some of the positive traits that I gleaned from others were learning how to understand and deal with people, as well as being able to read them. I have attempted to put myself in their shoes and then communicate to them what they needed to know. I also tried to determine what was important to them. I know that the traits that my parents have instilled in me went a long way in helping me to understand others.

My sisters, other friends, and associates also helped me understand how to communicate without getting "tipped over." By this I mean not losing your professional presence and to replace it with an irrational and emotional mindset, which does not appropriately evaluate every situation. I feel that you need to have a balance in how you learn things, as well as a curiosity. To be successful I believe you must maintain a professional presence. In the end, it has been my faith and trust in people that has allowed much more to be accomplished than I could have done alone.

I have always had a thirst for doing different things and getting others involved. I have always had some very interesting friends, who went down some different but interesting paths, which may have been out of my comfort zone. But these different or diverse relationships were very beneficial. Sometimes going to an opera enhances your knowledge and your depth, while if left to your own devices; you would not participate in such an activity out of your comfort zone.

If you look at growth from a company standpoint, as well as my own, our success has come from hard work and several other factors including care for the customer, technical innovation, and a focus on quality and performance. I can definitely attribute a lot of my success to my parents, as my dad was a workaholic, working 7 days a week and dedicated to whatever he was doing. I probably learned how to enjoy myself a little more than he did. I have taken the opportunity to become more involved in other things than work, such as sports activities. My mother had a very easy going nature about her; she was everyone's friend. My dad was much more intense. My dad was always much more focused on the job, but both brought to me different but useful habits and characteristics, that had a huge influence on my capacity to handle pressure, serving me well in my career.

One example of my dad's intensity may be better understood by the following anecdote. Two of my friends and I went up north with my dad, to paint our hunting cabin, which is located in the middle of "nowhere." This cabin is only seen by a handful of people, who may happen to come across it, deep in the woods. We were all busy painting, with our buckets and our brushes. Periodically, my dad would make the round to inspect our work, to be sure that it was up to his standards. As time progressed, my dad disqualified each of us from painting, one by one. In the end, my buddies and I were out on the lake fishing, while my dad finished the painting project by himself. He was very particular about quality and workmanship.

At Link, we continually look for ways to improve and enhance our systems through technical innovation and new designs. The world of testing is continually driven by the need to expand capabilities in order to keep up with product enhancements which push the envelope of performance, capabilities, and capacities.

I have personally engaged myself in a number of organizations and associations in the business and technical arena. These connections have allowed me to encounter many highly accomplished individuals who have taught me a great deal about being successful. With my educational foundation in technology and my exposure to business through my MBA training and work experience, I feel that I have been able to utilize learned skills and critical information to improve my business acumen, which has resulted in many positive experiences.

Of course, the focus on quality and workmanship in our products has always been a requirement to perpetuate the reputation of Link throughout our customer base. People are always willing to pay more when quality is not an issue. In the end, it is the people that buy our products and it is the personal interaction which allows for successful outcomes. From a personal standpoint, I have simply been blessed to have wonderful people all around me.

Sometimes I have to shake my head to find out how I have encountered such a large number of people in my life that have become really good friends. I have friends today that I went to kindergarten with, which I continue to stay in contact with, and that have become successful. Having stayed in the Detroit area all my life and being able to work here, vacation up north and other places that I go to, has enabled me to cultivate some long standing relationships that have worked out well. I think that is also part of my upbringing, where I resonate with many people with common interests. When you engage with someone that you have been able to develop a relationship with, this then enables you to develop a closeness which fosters compatibility. This in turn will optimize people's productivity. People having certain characteristics enable you to make friends with them.

If you have that type of connection, even if you have not seen that person for a long period of time, it develops a bond which allows you to start right back where you left off years ago. And so maybe part of the reason that we can get back together, is not where I want to take credit, it is just that long standing relationships afford a person opportunities. Having people reach out to me, guide me, as well as provide me opportunities, has helped me and Link, as I have travelled around the world. I have frequently become very closely engaged with customers who I truly consider as my friends. It has been very beneficial and gratifying to have the opportunity to work with people, both in and out of

Link, that are my friends. These work and social relationships all fit together for success.

For example, several years ago we sold a Dynamometer to test brakes to a major company in China. Due to shipping delays, the project didn't get completed until after the Letter of Credit had expired. This precluded them from making the last 10% ($100,000) payment. Because of our solid personal relationship with the customer, I received a message from my friend two years later, saying that if we could get an invoice to them immediately they would send the money, and that is what happened.

As much as I may have done, there is always much more that could be done, to give back to others. The need to help is never ending. I have involved myself in a variety of endeavors that I hope contribute to improving the lives of others.

I am a strong believer in developing and promoting technical professions and education. I feel that the technical profession is critical to the well-being of our society. This is particularly true in the US where innovation is depended upon to create the social and economic solutions necessary to maintain our way of life. I have participated in the Engineering Society of Detroit since 1971. This involvement has included a variety of positions within the Society, including Chair of the Young Engineers Council, membership, finance, facilities, awards, events, and President of the Society. We have promoted the technical community with programs for grade school and high school students, University Students, Young Engineers and Senior Engineers. I currently serve as Chairman of the Rackham Foundation which provides resources to the Engineering Society

213

of Detroit to carry out their good works. I have received a number of awards from the ESD including Distinguished Service, Outstanding Leadership and the Horace H. Rackham Humanitarian Award.

I served for 10 years on the Board of the Original Equipment Suppliers Association (OESA) which promotes the interests of the suppliers to the automotive industry. The OESA engages OEMs and legislators to look out for the best interests of our industry. The OESA also promotes students in technical fields, young engineers in their growth cycle, and both companies and individuals with critical information to help them navigate the issues, which challenge them on a daily basis.

Link Engineering personnel, as well as myself, participate in a number of industry organizations to help regulate and disperse critical technical information to improve each company's ability to compete and become better corporate citizens. This includes the Motor Equipment Manufacturers Association (MEMA) and their affiliates Brake Manufacturers Council (BMC) and Heavy Duty Brake Manufacturers Council (HDBMC). Issues such as copper in brake pads and reduced stopping distances are topics which have been addressed by the regulatory bodies to improve braking systems used in service. These organizations represent the industry point of view, and benefit from the involvement of me and others to resolve issues.

On an international level, we have contributed extensively to organizations such as ISO, JASO, CFSMA and others, to navigate the technical and economic issues, to bring Braking standards to an acceptable level worldwide.

I have been very deeply involved in numerous activities related to the Society of Automotive Engineers (SAE). I have participated and chaired many committees to improve upon testing standards within the automotive industry. I have spoken at events around the world to promote better testing protocols and thereby improve quality and performance of Braking systems worldwide. I chair the annual SAE Brake Colloquium, which brings together braking experts from around the world, to discuss how to improve Brakes and Braking performance.

I am on the Advisory Board for the Engineering School at Michigan State University to help guide the education of engineering students to be more applicable to the needs of our industries and communities. I am dedicated to promoting kids in technology worldwide.

With regards to mentoring, it hasn't been a formal structure with me, but more of a casual engagement. I keep track of certain people that I want to want to keep close to and monitor their progress. What I do typically, is have frequent conversations and discussions with them. This would include sharing ideas with them as well as encouraging their growth. I may or may not have had that much impact on their success, but every little bit helps.

What I try to do is give a person an opportunity to succeed and put people together that can do things better. There are some very talented people that just can't work with others and so their contributions seem to never come to fruition because of the relationship. What I have also found, is that if you can identify the leaders, they can heal wounds

215

that were opened up in an organization. Sometimes you just have to find a focal point to bring people together.

I also support Cornerstone Schools in the education of underprivileged elementary and high school students. Cornerstone is a Charter School within the City of Detroit. They have established a very comprehensive set of educational and extracurricular training vehicles to raise the students to new heights of achievement. They build a great deal of confidence within each of their students.

Their Mentoring Program involves quarterly visits with the students to witness their progress, spend a few hours with them, and provide personal encouragement. As the kids age, there are higher levels of involvement.

I provide donations to a variety of other charitable organizations to assist in their work to improve the lives of others. This enables individuals that may not have an economic opportunity to go forward and reach their goals. I do not really look at this as a charitable activity, but as helping to build a foundation for growth and prosperity.

Life is filled with diversity of experiences and opportunities. It is critical to keep your awareness of the circumstances that surround you and the individuals that are involved to be able to attain the highest level of accomplishment. Like a football team, everyone has a position to play. The ability of each individual to perform at his position and the ability of management to coordinate these individual positions into a team is what determines the accomplishments of the entire organization.

**Business Field:** Attorney - Judge
**Rupert Ruppert**
**Business Name:** Ruppert, Bronson & Ruppert Co., L.P.A.
**Court:** Franklin Municipal Court, Franklin, Ohio
**Position Held:** Judge of Franklin, Ohio Municipal Court

## Personal Background:

Rupert Ruppert was born in Franklin, Ohio. His mother and father were Paul and Elizabeth Rupert. He had 9 brothers and sisters. Rupert's children include:

Jason, 42; Ryan, 40; Bradley, 39; and Matthew 36. Stepdaughters: Beth, 32; Kelly 27
Rupert attended Franklin High School and graduated in 1961.

Further education included:

- 1963-1967: Army ROTC - Ohio State University
- Ohio State University, Bachelor of Arts Degree - BA 1968
- Capital University School of Law, Juris Doctorate Degree - JD 1976

While in high school, Rupert was elected President of the Senior Class. He was elected primarily because people seemed to like him, his leadership skills, and he was very easy to get along with. A lot of people are elected to governmental positions because people like them. It's not necessarily a criteria or known as to whether that person will do a great job. It's hoped once they take office they will succeed in their endeavors.

Rupert played Varsity Basketball his Junior and Senior years. Rupert played football his freshman year as a middle linebacker. But when he entered high school, the coach told him that he wanted to switch him to running back. Rupert thought that the problem was that there were a large number of good and even great running backs in those positions. It was obvious to Rupert that he was not really that fast, although maybe a little "shifty." In all likelihood Rupert probably would not get to play in front of the great runners they already had. Rupert determined he would be wasting his time and therefore decided not to play. He commented that he regrets his decision to this day.

Shortly after graduating from high school, Rupert began working at Laynecrest Lanes, the local bowling alley. He was an assistant manager. Also at that time, Rupert carried mail for the US Post Office on a part-time basis.

After working for 2 years, Rupert enrolled at the Ohio State University. He was elected to the Freshman Senate and Student Senate. He was on Student Senate a majority of the time at Ohio State. He was also the Ohio State University Bowling Champion for 2 years. Rupert thought that he was never a great athlete because he never worked hard enough to really be good. But, bowling came to him naturally.

After graduation from Ohio State in 1968, Rupert went into the Army as a 2$^{nd}$ Lieutenant and was stationed at Fort Bliss, Texas. While there, he received his orders to South Viet Nam to be an Infantry Advisor to the South Vietnamese Infantry. Rupert received his training for Viet Nam at Fort

Bragg, North Carolina, the home of the 82$^{nd}$ Airborne. He was trained by Green Berets and Vietnamese Veteran officers. Rupert said although he was successful, he didn't make a huge difference in the Viet Nam War in general, nor did any other individual.

Rupert stated that he had a great relationship with his Vietnamese counterparts. He was there to train them to conduct military strikes on the ground, as well as calling in airstrikes. This facilitated Army medivacs to evacuate wounded soldiers. He was involved in field operations on a fairly routine basis, out in the countryside looking for the enemy. They were known as "search and destroy missions." Rupert was promoted to 1$^{st}$ Lieutenant, where he earned the Combat Infantry Badge and the Bronze Star, while in Viet Nam.

Rupert left for Columbus, Ohio shortly after getting back from the war and entered Capital University Law School where he attended the night program. During this time he also began his first job in government service. This first job was in the Governor's office as head of the advance team wherein he assigned individuals to travel with Governor John J. Gilligan. In this position, Rupert had the good fortune to meet a lot of successful people. A number of them were in politics, such as senators, governors, congressmen and others. Since Rupert worked directly with the Governor and traveled with him most of the time, this opportunity afforded him a privilege to meet these types of people.

It was his responsibility, and those of the advance men working under him, to make certain that an event went smoothly, that everything was in place and that the event was successful. That would also mean that there would be no surprises for the Governor.

Rupert estimated that he traveled out of Columbus approximately 50% of the time. While traveling, he was exposed to almost all the Democrat and Republican officeholders in the State. While working in the Governor's office, he earned his law degree in 1976. Rupert said that something that surprises a lot of people. Rupert did not use any of the political relationships later in his life, to advance his own career. I am not sure that everyone can say that!

After graduating from law school, he came back to practice law with his brother, James D. Rupert, at the Rupert law offices in Franklin, Ohio. Rupert practiced law from 1976 to 1982 when he took a 9 month sabbatical to work as Deputy Campaign Manager for Attorney General William J. Brown. Brown was defeated in the gubernatorial primary by the future Governor, Richard Celeste. His main duties as Deputy Campaign Manager were to travel with the Attorney General and assist in briefings, planning, advertising, and communications with the main headquarters in Columbus.

After completing the primary Governor's race in 1982, Rupert went back to the private practice of law. He pointed out that the law field, like all other professions, had good attorneys, mediocre ones, and bad ones. He said that you learn from all of them. If you are with an attorney who is not as qualified as others, you will see that and learn from the mistakes he or she makes. The really good attorneys are the ones you strive to be around and to compete against. Working against a great attorney improves your own skills as an attorney.

When Rupert went back to Franklin and started practicing law, he was handling all kinds of cases. Rupert stated that one of the advantages was that he was 33 years old at the time. His age and a great deal of life experiences over the younger attorneys, gave him a competitive edge. This opinion was based on younger attorneys who were graduating law school at approximately 25 years of age.

Rupert felt that he was always good on his feet and had been a very good speaker. Rupert has excellent stand up skills in the courtroom, in front of juries or individuals, and practiced general law for the most part. Rupert said he had one specialty of handling Eminent Domain cases as an Assistant Attorney General for 15 years. Eminent Domaine cases are those that the State files to appropriate land for roadways, bridges and other governmental projects.

Rupert thought that it was a lot of fun to try those cases because you had unlimited funds to prepare for the trial and hire the experts you really needed. Rupert said that one of the cases that he handled as an Assistant Attorney General was against the largest and best law firm in the City of Dayton. Testimony from the State's witnesses indicated that the value of the taking was $90,000. The defendant's law firm argued and put on evidence that the loss to the property owner was in excess of $1,300,000. The jury came in at slightly above

$90,000. He said that was fairly typical in his work as an Assistant Attorney General and never had what was known as a quotient verdict. That's a verdict where the jury splits the difference between the State's case and the individual's case. All of the verdicts were less and most of the time considerably less that the 50% mean.

In 1986, due to Rupert's experience in statewide politics, he was named Senator John Glenn's (astronaut) statewide campaign manager. Senator Glenn won re-election that year by a sizeable margin. Again, Rupert traveled the state making new friends and political allies.

Rupert's brother, Judge James D. Rupert, was Franklin Municipal Court Judge from 1985 to 2005 when he retired. Rupert ran for election in 2005 and was elected Municipal Judge. Since then, he has been elected to a second term and will serve as the Municipal Judge until the end of 2017.

As a Municipal Court Judge, he says that success is predicated upon your effectiveness, fairness, and economically running the Court, but also in treating people who come into the courtroom with dignity and respect. Rupert would see anywhere from 80 to 120 people per week in his courtroom. This was over the last 10 years, and not once has he ever had a disturbance or a problem, with a defendant in the courtroom. He pointed out that when people came to court, obviously, it was not the best day of their life. However, if the defendants in the courtroom are treated kindly and with respect, then there should be no problem.

Rupert said that anyone charged with a crime for which they may be jailed is entitled to a jury trial.

However, he said that in the 10 years as Judge, he had probably not had more than 2 or 3 jury trials in any given year. Rupert stated that the reason for that was that the attorneys knew that they would get a "fair shake" with Judge Rupert sitting on the bench. They knew that the Rupert wouldn't do crazy things in relationship to sentencing and that he was reasonable. Attorneys acknowledged that Rupert was tough when he had to be, but very moderate most of the time, with people who have not committed serious offenses.

Rupert stated that the Court handles approximately 2,000 criminal cases each year in addition to approximately 4,000 traffic cases. Rupert said that it is the responsibility of the Judge to be fair, honest, compassionate, and hard-nosed when needed. In addition, the Judge needs to be a good listener to hear what the defendants have to say because often times, their illegal acts may have come at very difficult times in their lives or under very difficult circumstances.

A good Judge has to look at all those factors to determine what punishment is appropriate. One of Rupert's rules is that if someone has been physically hurt by the defendant, then the defendant goes to jail. Also, the court looks at the number of prior convictions of criminal offenses and if there are a substantial number, then the time they serve in jail is increased greatly.

Rupert said that although a person is charged with theft, assault, or domestic violence, the facts vary from case to case. For instance, he stated that if someone is caught stealing diapers and food for a child and they don't have a job, then that particular case is different from the person who steals a number of CD's for resale so they can support a drug habit. The first example deserves to be treated with dignity and respect and receive a moderate sentence, whereas the career criminals and those who have committed multiple crimes in the past must be treated much more harshly. Rupert stated there are a lot of judges who will treat a first time offender, who has no prior record, with harsh punishment.

Rupert pointed out one has to look at each case that comes to you; that hard and fast rules just don't always work. The circumstances change from case to case. Rupert said that if someone is unemployed, down and out, having family issues, mental health issues, or other problems, you have to take that into consideration when sentencing an individual. He said, "At least I do."

Rupert has had a successful career. In addition to being Judge, Rupert was chosen as Franklin Area Citizen of the Year in 1993, was President of the Warren County Bar Association, President of the Franklin Rotary Club, Chairman of the Franklin Pool Board, Chairman of the Joint Emergency Medical Services, Chairman of the Warren County Democratic Party and many others.

Rupert thought that his success could be attributed to his education, hard work, honesty, thoughtfulness and treating everyone as you would like to be treated. He stated that a person needs to keep themselves grounded. They shouldn't brag about their accomplishments and should never believe that they are really special. Rupert stated that one of the reasons for his success was that if he made a commitment, he kept it. He served on literally dozens of Boards and Commissions, in addition to those cited above, and was actively involved in each and every one of them. In fact, if you took the combined number of years of all the boards and commissions that he served on since 1980, it totaled up to 79 years of service.

Finally, Rupert thought that it was important for people who are successful in life to give back to their community. As set forth above, he has been involved in many boards and commissions, charitable organizations and other state, city or countywide endeavors. He felt that a person should give his best, not only to his family, but to his community.

## Tim & Robin Weidle
**Business Names:** Real Estate/Development
**Business Names:** Lutgert Companies/Premier Sotheby's International Realty
**Current Positions:** Realtors

## Personal Backgrounds:
### Tim Weidle:

I grew up on a nursery owned by my parents. I worked in the nursery while attending school. Duties included everything involved with having a nursery; cultivating trees, planting, hoeing, trimming, digging, and selling. There was a lot of hard labor, but lessons learned from these experiences paid off well in the future.

After graduating from Franklin High School in Ohio, I obtained a BS degree from Ohio State University and then earned a MS degree from Xavier University. During that time, my work experiences varied considerably. They included working in the nursery and a paper mill, driving a tanker truck for Mobil Oil, and doing "odd jobs" to earn money for our Florida vacations.

Following completion of college, my careers were in the educational, real estate, insurance, and marketing fields. Some people humorously claimed that I could not hold a job; but little did I know that all of these different "occupations" were building blocks to my future success.

After growing up and living in the same area for over 40 years, Robin and I decided to "follow our dream" and relocate to Florida in 1986. Here we were in our forties with 2 children still in school, selling everything and moving to Florida to begin "new" careers. Imagine how scary! I began working in the construction industry; with no professional experience, I started as a laborer and came home more than a few days being tired, hot, and sweaty. I kept thinking, "Did we make the right decision?" As I gained experience in the industry, I became involved in the development of luxury high-rise condominiums, finally ascending to the position of Vice President of Residential Development.

Recently I have joined my wife, working as a team for Premier Sotheby's International Realty specializing in marketing luxury homes and condominiums.

### Robin Weidle:

I also graduated from Franklin High School and attended Miami of Ohio in Oxford. I worked for Armco Steel Corporation for 22 years and held various positions in the human resource area. After moving to Naples, Florida I worked for a bank in the trust area. I then obtained my real estate license and became involved in the marketing of luxury real estate in Naples.

### Commentaries:
### We believe that ethics and success go "hand-in-hand."

Our families were very similar, they raised us to be honest and treat everyone with respect. We were both brought up knowing the value of working for the things we wanted. Our prior work ethics provided us the understanding to realize that most things in life are *not given*, but *earned.*

Our ancestors believed in giving back to others. We follow that same practice. Whenever we receive a referral, we show our appreciation with a gift to the referrer. It does not have to be large in nature; it is the thought that counts. Our children are practicing this belief. For example, a dear friend of ours died and left our children in his will. They signed their part of the inheritance to his spouse because she meant so much to them.

Being truthful and earning trust has been ingrained in us. We found that these attributes promote better working relationships with others and encourage them to reciprocate. As a project manager, Tim frequently had very influential customers who expected things that were not necessarily obtainable. These people were not used to hearing and/or accepting "no" for an answer. He found the best solution was to quickly and honestly explain why what they wanted might not be probable and proceeded to provide them with other avenues for accomplishing their wishes.

We work together in creating our marketing strategy and attend training classes to keep abreast of the latest rules, laws, and marketing techniques in order to better serve our customers. We also strive to keep them informed as quickly as possible and follow up with them in a timely manner. Going that "extra mile" will make a positive and memorable impression.

The two of us use our own specific strengths as a team to assist our customers. Robin has a great personality for meeting new customers and relates well with most anyone. She does not know a stranger. She has extensive knowledge of the various forms required to prepare listings, contracts, amendments, etc. Because of my construction background and experience in the geographical area we serve, I am able to answer many customer questions and resolve their issues.

We live in a society today with a lot of challenges. We must "practice what our ancestors preached" and strive to *work hard and set a proud example to those who follow.*

# Epilogue

What I have attempted to do, is bring to you the reader, some information and understanding of the concept of "Success," and how it may or may not be defined.

Have I changed your opinion of whom you might know who is successful on a local level, but not a national level? Are these local people any less successful, because they are not that well known, is up for discussion among you and your friends.

A concept that I learned about in the previous chapters support a concept called "Present State vs Future State." By this I mean, if we take a look at where we are today, determine where we want to be in the next 6-18 months, we then need to determine what will help us get there versus what is hindering us from getting there. Once the hindrances or barriers to the "Future State" are known, we can come up with a game plan to turn those hindrances into positives, which will help us make this journey faster and more pleasurable.

Previously, I made a statement that I was looking for a "Common Thread" from successful people. It appears from the previous chapters that the term Common Thread may be plural. Some of the "Common Threads" may be one or more than one word:

- Church
- Relationship
- Community
- Parents
- Family

- Have a plan that aligns with professionals and mimic their positive behavior
- Watch, listen, and learn
- Show gratitude, which may be a form of giving back
- Both success and failure exist in the power of your mind
- A lot can be accomplished if you are not worried about who gets the credit. "Politicians, are you listening to this?"
- If you really want to know what a person believes in, be courteous and listen to what they say, but *most* importantly watch their behavior
- One of the toughest times to pray is when things are going well
- By the same token, it may be just as important to note the differences of successful people, as:
  - Economic background (Poor vs Economic stability)
  - Educational background (2nd grade education vs a Master's degree or an MD)
  - Number of parents (2 vs 1 parent)

Think about it, how many of us have lived out of a car or slept on a thin mattress in a closet and still became a "Success?" Is there really a recipe for "Success?" There appear to be a lot of different roads to get there.

In the preceding chapters, there has been a lot of "text" that different people have used to describe their Success. Me, I am more of a "visual" person. Like the old saying goes, "A picture is worth a thousand words."

The picture above is a 1st place medal that my granddaughter Isabella won, at the Green Lake Spring Regatta. Isabella, plus 8 other crew members were a rowing team that won this medal. I know nothing about a rowing competition. But one thing that I do know, is that all of the crew members have to work together and be in unison to compete, much less win.

Finally, I hope that you have enjoyed and can really take something away from what was presented. I know that I have gained a lot of insight into what makes some folks "Successful" and some not. If you, the reader, can *apply* any of the information that I have presented, that will make me "Successful."

## About the Author

Jim Villella was born and raised in Franklin, Ohio, a small southwest Ohio town located between Dayton and Cincinnati.

After graduating from Franklin High School in 1962, he enlisted in the United States Air Force and became an aircraft maintenance technician, or crew chief, as commonly called in that career field.

After his enlistment ended in 1966, Jim worked a year as a laborer in the construction trade. During this year he also worked as a laborer at Armco Steel Corporation in Middletown, Ohio.

Deciding that being a laborer all of his life was not going to be the greatest occupation, Jim decided to enroll at Miami University, located in Oxford, Ohio. Jim graduated with a Bachelor of Science degree in Applied Science from Miami (Ohio) University in 1970.

Only with the help of his wife, the support of his mom and dad, his mother-in-law and father-in-law, and working as a gas station attendant (that actually put gas in your vehicle) in the evenings, was he able to complete his college degree.

After college graduation, Jim secured employment at a local General Motors plant in Dayton, Ohio as a Manufacturing Engineer. Thirty four years later, in 2004, Jim retired as a Delphi Corporation employee.

In 1988, during his tenure with GM, Jim decided to go into the Air Force Reserve located at

Wright-Patterson Base in Fairborn, Ohio. Sixteen years later, he retired from the Air Force Reserve as a Senior Master Sergeant in the area of aircraft maintenance.

Jim is co-author of the book *The Battle to Stay Competitive*, published by Productivity Press. He also has his own consulting firm, Villella and Co., LLC, which helps small manufacturing firms improve their competitive position.

Jim resides in Chandler, Arizona with his wife Kim and a 5 ½ month old cocker spaniel puppy named Gracie. Jim also has a daughter Jamie, son-in-law Charlie, granddaughter Isabella, and a grandson Harrison, that live on Bainbridge Island, Washington.